Mandela's Way

Mandela's Way

Lessons on Life

RICHARD STENGEL

Published by Virgin Books 2010

2 4 6 8 10 9 7 5 3 1

Copyright © Richard Stengel 2010

This edition published by arrangement with Crown Publishers, an imprint of the Crown
Publishing Group, a division of Random House, Inc.

Richard Stengel has asserted his right under the Copyright, Designs
and Patents Act 1988 to be identified as the author of this work

Design by Leonard W. Henderson

First published in Great Britain in 2010 by
Virgin Books
Random House, 20 Vauxhall Bridge Road,
London SW1V 2SA

www.virginbooks.com
www.rbooks.co.uk

Addresses for companies within The Random House Group Limited can be found at:
www.randomhouse.co.uk/offices.htm

The Random House Group Limited Reg. No. 954009

A CIP catalogue record for this book
is available from the British Library

Hardback ISBN 9781905264773
Trade paperback ISBN 9780753519332

The Random House Group Limited supports The Forest Stewardship Council
[FSC], the leading international forest certification organisation. All our titles that
are printed on Greenpeace-approved FSC-certified paper carry the FSC logo.
Our paper procurement policy can be found at www.rbooks.co.uk/environment

Mixed Sources
Product group from well-managed
forests and other controlled sources
www.fsc.org Cert no. TT-COC-2139
© 1996 Forest Stewardship Council
FSC

Printed and bound in Great Britain by
CPI Mackays, Chatham, Kent, ME5 8TD

For Anton and Gabriel

Contents

Contents

Preface

In Africa there is a concept known as *ubuntu*—
the profound sense that we are human only through the
humanity of others; that if we are to accomplish anything in this world, it will in equal measure be due to the
work and achievements of others. Richard Stengel is one
of those people who readily grasps this idea. He is an
outstanding writer with a deep understanding of our
history. We are enormously grateful to him for his col-
laboration on the creation of *Long Walk to Freedom*. We
have fond memories of the many hours of conversation
and hard work we put in together on that project. He
has shown remarkable insight into the many complex
leadership challenges still facing the world today and all
the individuals in it. Everyone can learn from it.

—Nelson Mandela, November 2008

A Complex Man

WE LONG FOR HEROES but have too few. Nelson Mandela is perhaps the last pure hero on the planet. He is the smiling symbol of sacrifice and rectitude, revered by millions as a living saint. But this image is one-dimensional. He would be the first to tell you that he is far from a saint—and that is not false modesty.

Nelson Mandela is a man of many contradictions. He is thick-skinned but easily wounded. He is sensitive to how others feel but often ignores those closest to him. He is generous with money but counts his pennies when giving a tip. He will not step on a cricket or spider but was the first commander of the African National Congress's military wing. He is a man of the people but revels in the company of celebrities. He is eager to please but not afraid to say no. He doesn't like to take credit, but will let you know when he should get it. He shakes the hands of everyone in the kitchen but doesn't know all of his bodyguards' names.

His persona is a mixture of African royalty and British aristocracy. He is a Victorian gentleman in a silk dashiki. His manners are courtly—after all, he learned them in colonial British schools from headmasters who read Dickens when Dickens was still writing. He is formal: He will bow slightly and hold out his arm for you to go first. But he is not the least bit finicky or prim—he will talk in almost clinical detail about the toilet routine in prison on Robben Island or how it felt when his foreskin was sliced off in his tribal circumcision ritual at the age of sixteen. He will use fancy silverware when he is in London or Johannesburg, but when he is in his home area of the Transkei he enjoys eating with his hands, as is the local custom.

Nelson Mandela is meticulous. He takes tissues from a box and refolds them individually before placing them in his front pocket. I have seen him remove his shoe during an interview to reverse one sock when he notices it is inside out. In prison, he made a fair copy of every letter he wrote over two decades, and kept a detailed list of every letter he received, with the date he got it and when he replied. Until his marriage to Graça Machel, he slept on one side of his king-size bed, while the other side remained pristine and untouched. He rises before dawn and makes his bed precisely every morning, whether he is at home or in a hotel. I have seen the look of shock on hotel housekeepers when they find him making the bed. He hates to be late and regards lack of punctuality as a character flaw.

I've never known a human being who can be as still as Nelson Mandela. When he is sitting or listening, he does not tap his fingers or his foot, or move about. He has no nervous tics. When I have adjusted his tie or smoothed his jacket or fixed a microphone on his lapel, it was like fussing with a statue. When he listens to you, it is as though you are looking at a still photograph of him. You would barely know he was breathing.

He is a power charmer—confident that he will charm you, by whatever means possible. He is attentive, courtly, winning, and, to use a word he would hate, seductive. And he works at it. He will learn as much as he can about you before meeting you. When he was first released, he would read journalists' pieces and praise them individually with specific details. And like most great charmers, he himself is easily charmed—you can accomplish that by letting him see that he has won you over.

The charm is political as well as personal. Politics is ultimately about persuasion, and he regards himself not so much as the Great Communicator but as the Great Persuader. He will either get you through logic and argument or through charm—and usually a combination of the two. He would always rather persuade you to do something than order you to do so. But he will order you to do so if he has to.

He wants to be liked. He likes to be admired. He hates to disappoint. He wants you to come away from meeting him thinking that he is everything you had ever hoped for. This requires tremendous energy, and he gives of himself to almost everyone he meets. Almost everyone gets the Full Mandela. Except when he is tired. Then his eyes droop to half-mast and he seems asleep on his feet. But I've never known a man to be so revived by a night's sleep. He can seem at death's door at ten P.M., but then eight hours later, at six A.M., he will seem sprightly and twenty years younger.

His charm is in inverse proportion to how well he knows you. He is warm with strangers and cool with intimates. That warm benign smile is bestowed on every new person who comes within his orbit. But the smile is reserved for outsiders. I saw him often with his son, his daughters, his sisters, and the Nelson Mandela they know often appears to be a stern and unsmiling fellow who is not terribly sympathetic to their problems. He is a Victorian/African father, not a modern one. When you ask him something he doesn't want to talk about, he will fix his face into a frown of displeasure. His mouth becomes an inverted cartoon of his smile. Do not try to force the issue or he will simply become stony and turn his attention elsewhere. When that happens, it is like a sunny day that has suddenly become overcast.

Mandela is indifferent to almost all material possessions—he does not know or care about the names of cars, couches, or watches—but I've seen him dispatch a bodyguard to drive an hour to get his favorite pen. He is generous with his children when it comes to money, but don't count on his generosity if you are his waiter. The two of us once had lunch at a fancy hotel restaurant in Johannesburg where he was waited on hand and foot. The bill came to well over one thousand rand, and I watched as Mandela examined some coins in his hand and left a few tiny pieces of change. After he had gone, I slipped a one-hundred-rand note to the waiter. It was not the only time I ever did so.

He will always stand up for what he believes is right with a stubbornness that is virtually unbending. I very often heard him say, "This isn't right." Whether it concerned something mundane or of international importance, his tone was unvarying. I heard him say it when a security guard's key would not open his office, and I heard him say it directly to South African President F. W. de Klerk about the constitutional negotiations. He used the phrase for years on Robben Island when talking to a guard or the head of the prison. *This isn't right.* In a very basic way, this intolerance of injustice was what

goaded him. It was the engine of his discontent, his simple verdict on the basic immorality of apartheid. He saw
something wrong and tried to right it. He saw injustice
and tried to fix it.

✳   ✳   ✳

How do I know all of this?

I collaborated with Nelson Mandela on his autobiography. We worked together for nearly three years, and
during much of that time I saw him almost every day. I
traveled with him, ate with him, tied his shoes, straightened his tie—and spent hours and hours in conversation
with him about his life and work.

My path to Mandela was an accidental one. I first
went to South Africa by chance: I took the place of another journalist who canceled his trip at the last minute.
Based on that trip, I wrote a book about small-town life
in South Africa under apartheid. When the editor of
Mandela's memoir-to-be stumbled across my book, he
offered me the chance to work with Mandela on his life
story.

That's how I found myself in Johannesburg in December of 1992, waiting to meet Nelson Mandela. It
was a difficult, treacherous time in South African his-

tory; the country was in danger of descending into civil war. Mandela had been out of prison for less than three years and was struggling to consolidate his power, and move the country toward the first democratic elections in its history. Working on his autobiography was not exactly number one on his "to do" list—but he wanted to tell his story.

He kept me waiting for nearly a month before our first meeting. And when we finally met, I almost capsized the project. I was sitting in the anteroom outside his old office in ANC headquarters, waiting for him to emerge. Instead, I looked up and he was headed down the hallway toward me from the other direction. He walked slowly, in a controlled, almost slow-motion way. The first thing I noticed was his skin—it's a beautiful caramel color, a soft, yellowish brown. His features are beautifully molded, with high cheekbones and an almost Asian cast. He is six-foot-two, and everything about him—his head, his hands—seems a little larger than life. As he came closer, I stood up.

"Ah, you must be . . ." he said, and then waited for me to fill in the blank.

"Richard Stengel," I said, and he put out his hand. It was fleshy, warm, and dry; his fingers as thick as sausages, the skin still rough from decades of hard labor.

He looked me over. "Ah," he said with a smile, "you are a young man." The last two words were pronounced as one: *youngman*. This was clearly not a compliment. He gestured for me to come into his office. It was large and formal and completely tidy. It looked like a show office but it was not. He paused to have a word with his assistant, a brisk, tiny woman who handed him a paper to sign. He took the paper slowly and deliberately; it was obvious that he did everything in a very deliberate way. Then he sat down at his desk and began to read it. He wasn't scanning it, he was reading it—every word. He then wrote his name slowly at the bottom, as though he was still perfecting his signature.

He walked over and sat in the well-worn leather chair opposite the couch. He asked me when I had arrived. His voice was slightly foggy, like a trumpet with a mute on it.

"Did you come over just for this project or for something else as well?" he asked.

My heart sank. His question implied that the autobiography was not quite enough to justify a trip on its own. I said I had come solely for the book. He nodded. He does not waste words.

He told me that he was planning on going on holiday on December 15, and that his staff had set aside four or five days for us to talk. He added that he hoped we could finish the project before his vacation, which was ten days away. I had spent a month of making unanswered calls trying to see him and several months of preparation and research, so it was perhaps the pent-up frustration that led me to say to him, in a slightly raised voice, "Four or five days? If you think you can produce this book in four or five sessions, you're . . . you're"—I could not think of the right word—"*deluding* yourself."

I had been in Mandela's presence for less than ten minutes and I had suggested that he did not have a firm grip on reality. He regarded me with a slightly raised eyebrow and then stood up. He was ready for me to go. He then walked back to his desk, buzzed his assistant, and said, "Mr. Stengel is here and we are trying to work out a schedule." He said that he had an engagement that evening and that he didn't mean to rush me, but that I should speak to his assistant on Monday morning. With that, I was out of his office—and perhaps, out of his life.

The following Monday evening, I received a call that Mandela would see me at seven the next morning. Promptly at seven, we sat in the same configuration as last time. "Let's begin," he said, as though he were a judge getting ready to launch a trial. I cleared my throat and said that I first wanted to apologize for my behavior the other day. "I'm sorry I was so, so . . ." and I paused, again at a loss for the right word, "so *brusque* with you the other day." The word sounded foreign and pretentious. He looked at me and smiled—a smile that was amused, understanding, and a little weary.

"You must be a very gentle young man indeed," he said, "if you thought our conversation the other day was *brusque.*" And he said the word very deliberately, with a trilled *r* at the beginning and a hard *q* at the end.

I laughed.

He had been in prison for twenty-seven years with guards who, for much of that time, treated him as less than human and with a casual brutality that he took for granted. Before that he had been hunted by policemen and soldiers who regarded him as a terrorist to be stopped at all costs. He lived in a country where the white ruling class did not consider him or treat him as a full human being. All of that was a little more than brusque.

And that was the beginning of our friendship. Over the next two years, I amassed more than seventy hours of interviews with him, but that paled in comparison to the hours, days, and months we spent in each other's company. I decided early on I would be at his side as much as he could tolerate—at meetings, events, holidays, and state trips. I spent hours with him at his home in Houghton, I traveled with him to his country home in the Transkei, and went with him to America and Europe and elsewhere in Africa. I campaigned with him, I went to negotiation sessions with him, I became, as much as I could, his shadow. I kept a diary of my time with him that eventually grew to 120,000 words. Much of this book comes from those notes.

Anyone who has spent much time with Nelson Mandela knows that it is not only a great privilege but a great pleasure. His presence is golden, luminous. You feel a little taller, a little finer. Most of the time, he is upbeat, confident, generous, fun. Even when the weight of the world was on his shoulders, he would wear it lightly. When you are with him, you feel you are living history as it is being made. He let me inside much of his life, some of his thoughts, and a little bit of his heart. He became the man who urged me to marry the South African woman who became my wife, and he eventually became godfather to my first son. I loved him. He was the cause of so many of the best things that have happened in my own life. When I left his side when the book was finally completed, it was like the sun going out of my life. We have seen each other many times over the years, and he has spent time with my two boys, who regard him as a kindly old grandfather. But he is no longer a regular presence in our lives. This book is both a thank-you for the time and affection he gave me and a gift to others who were unable to receive the benefit of his generosity and wisdom.

✳   ✳   ✳

Nelson Mandela had many teachers in his life, but the greatest of them all was prison. Prison molded the man we see and know today. He learned about life and leadership from many sources: from his rather distant father; from the king of the Thembu, who raised him like a son; from his stalwart friends and colleagues Walter Sisulu and Oliver Tambo; from historical figures and heads of state like Winston Churchill and Haile Selassie; from the words of Machiavelli and Tolstoy. But the twenty-seven years he spent in prison became the crucible that both hardened him and burned away all that was extraneous. Prison taught him self-control, discipline, and focus—the things he considers essential to leadership—and it taught him how to be a full human being.

The Nelson Mandela who emerged from prison at seventy-one was a different man from the Nelson Mandela who went in at forty-four. Listen to this description of the young Mandela by his closest friend and one-time law partner, Oliver Tambo, who became the head of the ANC while Mandela was in prison: "As a man, Nelson Mandela is passionate, emotional, sensitive, quickly stung to bitterness and retaliation by insult and patronage."

Emotional? Passionate? Sensitive? Quickly stung? The Nelson Mandela who emerged from prison is none of those things, at least on the surface. Today he would find all of those adjectives objectionable. Indeed, one of the sharpest criticisms he ever levels at anyone is that they are "emotional" or "too passionate" or "sensitive." Time and again the words I heard him use to praise others were "balanced," "measured," "controlled." The praise we give others is a reflection of how we perceive ourselves—and those are precisely the words he would use to describe himself.

How did this passionate revolutionary become a measured statesman? In prison, he had to temper his responses to everything. There was little a prisoner could control. The one thing you could control—that you *had* to control—was yourself. There was no room for outbursts or self-indulgence or lack of discipline. He had no zone of privacy. When I first walked into Mandela's old cell on Robben Island, I gasped. It's not a human-sized space, much less Mandela-sized. He could not stretch out when he was lying down. It was obvious that prison had, both literally and figuratively, molded him: There was no room for extraneous motion or emotion; everything had to be pruned away; everything had to be ordered. Every morning and every evening, he painstakingly arranged the few possessions that he was allowed in that tiny cell.

At the same time, he had to stand up every day to the authorities. He was the leader of the prisoners and could not let his side down; everyone saw or knew instantly if you backed down or compromised. He became even more acutely aware of how he was perceived by his colleagues. Though he was sequestered from the wider world, prison was its own universe, and he had to lead there as much as or more than when he emerged. And amid all this, he had time—far too much time—to think and plan and refine, and then refine some more. For twenty-seven years, he pondered not only policy, but how to behave, how to be a leader, how to be a man.

Mandela is not introspective—at least not in the sense that he will talk about his inner feelings or thoughts. He often became frustrated—and sometimes irritated—when I tried to get him to analyze his feelings. He is not fluent in the modern language of psychology or self-help. The world in which he was raised was unaffected by Sigmund Freud. He broods a great deal on the past, but he rarely talks about it. There was only one moment of self-pity I ever saw. We were talking about his childhood, and he looked off into the distance and said, "I am an old man who can only live in the past." And this was at a time when he was getting ready to be president of the new South Africa and create a new nation—the moment of his greatest triumph.

Over and over, though, I used to ask him how prison had changed him. How was the man who came out in 1990 different from the man who entered in 1962? This question annoyed him. He either ignored it, went straight to a policy answer, or denied the premise. Finally, one day, he said to me in exasperation, "I came out mature."

I came out mature.

What did he mean by those words? André Malraux wrote in his memoirs that the rarest thing in the world is a mature man. Mandela would agree with him. To me, those four words are the deepest clue to who Nelson Mandela is and what he learned. Because that sensitive, emotional young man did not go away. He is still inside the Nelson Mandela we see today. By maturity, he meant that he learned to control those more youthful impulses, not that he was no longer stung or hurt or angry. It is not that you always know what to do or how to do it, it is that you are able to tamp down the emotions and anxieties that get in the way of seeing the world as it is. You can see through them, and that will see you through.

At the same time, he realized that not everyone can be Nelson Mandela. Prison steeled him but it broke many others. Understanding that made him more empathetic, not less. He never lorded it over those who could not take it. He never blamed anyone for giving in. Surrendering was only human. Over the years, he developed a radar and a deep sympathy for human frailty. In some way, he was fighting for the right of every human being not to be treated the way he had been. He never lost that young man's softness or sensitivity; he just developed a harder and more invulnerable shell to protect it.

It is impossible to write about Nelson Mandela these days and not compare him to another potentially transformational black leader, Barack Obama. The parallels are many. I went to see Mandela during the Democratic presidential primaries last year and asked him whom he preferred, Hillary Clinton or Barack Obama. He smiled and then waved a finger at me in the universal gesture of, You're trying to get me in trouble. He would not answer. His restraint was characteristic.

That self-control, that omnipresent filter, is something the two men share. And while it took twenty-seven years in prison to mold the Nelson Mandela we know, the forty-eight-year-old American president seems to have achieved a Mandela-like temperament without the long years of sacrifice. Obama's self-discipline, his willingness to listen and to share credit, his inclusion of his rivals in his administration, and his belief that people want things explained, all seem like a twenty-first-century version of Mandela's values and persona. While Mandela's worldview was forged in the cauldron of racial politics, Obama is creating a post-racial political model. Whatever Mandela may or may not think of the new American president, Obama is in many ways his true successor on the world stage.

But Mandela's life is a model not just for our time but all time. The lessons you are about to read are those that I believe he learned not only in prison but over the course of his whole life. They are among the things that make him a leader and an exemplary human being. No, not everyone can be Nelson Mandela. He would tell you to be grateful for that. Fortunately, few of us have to endure in our own lives what he had to endure in his. But that does not mean these lessons are not applicable to our daily lives. They are. I know, because my life has been deepened by them. For Mandela, prison distilled the lessons of life and leadership, and I have attempted to do the same in this book. You can learn them at a fraction of the cost that he had to pay.

1

Courage Is Not the Absence of Fear

MOST PEOPLE WOULD SAY THAT Nelson Mandela personifies courage. But Mandela himself defines courage in a curious way. He does not see it as innate, or as a kind of elixir we can drink, or learned in any conventional way. He sees it as the way we *choose* to be. None of us is born courageous, he would say; it is all in how we react to different situations.

There were many moments in Mandela's life when he was tested. The ones people know about were large and public and dramatic. But courage, he would say, is an everyday activity, and we can display it in ways large and small. I had a glimpse into the nature of his courage in Natal in 1994. It was in the midst of the run-up to the first democratic South African election, when political violence was at epidemic levels. He chose to fly to Natal on a small propeller plane to give a speech to his Zulu supporters. He probably should not have gone at all. At the time, many of his Zulu supporters were being

23

murdered by the rival Zulu Inkatha Freedom Party and the situation was far from safe. But he was resolute.

I had agreed to meet his flight at the airport. When the plane was twenty minutes from landing, an airport official came over to me to say that one of the engines in the tiny plane had given out, and that they were planning on having fire engines and ambulances on the tarmac in case anything went wrong. The official said that in such cases, the pilot was usually able to land the plane without incident.

Mandela was on the plane with a lone bodyguard—Mike was his name—and two pilots. Twenty minutes later, surrounded by fire engines and ambulances, the plane made a slightly rocky landing. A smiling Nelson Mandela entered the small lounge, where he was besieged by a busload of Japanese tourists. True to form, Mandela was intent on shaking hands with each of them and posed with a great, big smile for whoever wanted a picture.

While Mandela posed, I huddled with Mike, who told me that two-thirds of the way through the trip, Mandela had leaned over to him, pointed out the window, and calmly said that the propeller did not seem to be working. He asked Mike to inform the pilots. Mike went to the cabin. The pilots knew full well about it and told him that they had called the airport and emergency landing procedures had been started. Most likely everything would be okay, they said. Mike told this to Mandela, who silently nodded and went back to reading his newspaper. Mike, who was not an experienced flier, said he himself was trembling with fear and that the only thing that calmed him was staring at Mandela, who continued to read the paper as though he were a suburban commuter on the morning train headed in to the office. Mike said Mandela barely looked up from the newspaper when the plane was making its landing.

When Mandela finished shaking hands, we were hustled into the backseat of the bulletproof BMW that would take us to the rally. I asked him how the flight was and he leaned over, opened his eyes very wide, and in a dramatic voice said, "Man, I was *terrified* up there!"

Though it may surprise people who know him only as an icon, I cannot tell you how many times he told me during our interviews that he had been scared. He was scared during the Rivonia Trial that sentenced him to life in prison; he was scared when wardens on Robben Island threatened to beat him; he was scared when he was an underground fugitive known in the press as the "Black Pimpernel"; he was scared when he secretly began negotiations with the government; and he was scared during the turbulent period before the election that would make him president of South Africa. He was never afraid to say he had been afraid.

His sense of courage was formed early. From when he was a small boy, Mandela heard tales of the bravery of such legendary African leaders as Dingane and Bambata and Makana. After his father died when he was nine, he was taken to a royal village called Mqhekezweni to be raised by Jongintaba, the king of the Thembu people. Mandela's father had been a local chief who was also a counselor to the king. The king wanted to groom young Nelson to be a counselor to his own son when he would become king. The king saw himself in a long line of African heroes and was devoted to following the traditional Xhosa rituals and ceremonies. One such ceremony haunted Mandela for the rest of his life.

In January 1934, when he was sixteen, he and twenty-five other boys of the same age were secluded in two grass huts on the banks of the Mbashe River. These were the elite boys of the village. Their bodies had been shaved clean, they were coated in white ocher, and wore only blankets over their shoulders. They looked like ghosts. Anxious and tense, they were getting ready for the Xhosa ritual of circumcision, what Mandela called the "essential step necessary in the life of every Xhosa male." This was not a private ritual, but a public one, and the king, a number of chiefs, and a crowd of friends and relatives were sitting by the side of the river. It was not only a rite of passage but a public test of courage. Each boy in turn was circumcised by an *ingcibi* (a circumcision expert). Here is Mandela's account of what happened, from his unpublished diary:

> Suddenly there was excitement and a thin elderly man shot past towards my left and squatted in front of the first boy. A few seconds thereafter I heard this boy say: *"Ndiyindoda!"* (I am a man!) Then Justice [the king's son and Mandela's best friend] repeated the word, followed one after the other by the three boys between us. The old man was moving fast and before I knew what was happening he was right in front of me. I looked straight into his eyes. He was deadly pale and though the day was cold, his face was shining with perspiration. Without saying a word he seized and pulled the foreskin and brought down the assegai. It was a perfect cut, clean and round like a ring. Within a week the wound healed, but without

anesthetic, the actual incision was as if molten lead was flowing through my veins. For seconds I forgot about the refrain and tried instead to absorb the shock of the assegai by digging my head and shoulders into a grass wall. I recovered and just managed to repeat the formula *"Ndiyindoda!"* (I am a man!) The other boys seemed much stronger and repeated the chorus promptly and clearly when each one's turn came round.

When he recounted this story for me, nearly sixty years after the wintry afternoon when it happened, Mandela was rueful, almost pained. And not because he was recalling the physical sensation of the operation, but because he believed that he had not reacted well. The pain of the procedure had died away, but not the pain of having been fainthearted. "I faltered," he said, looking down. "I did not yell it out in a firm voice." He felt that the other boys had been braver, stronger. He says he discovered that he was not naturally brave—perhaps none of us are—and that he would have to learn how to be so. He was disappointed in himself all those many years later, but the ritual had had its intended effect: He had resolved that he would always look strong, that he would never appear to falter.

※　※　※

In the early months of our interviews, when we were talking about his dealings with the police, or going underground, I would ask whether he had been afraid. He would look at me as though I was an ignoramus and say, "Of course I was afraid." Only a fool would not have been scared, he would say. But in each instance, he said, he did everything he could to tamp down his fear—he was simply unwilling to let anyone else see that he might be afraid.

Courage is not the absence of fear, he taught me. It's learning to overcome it.

In the 1950s, he once drove down to the Free State to see Dr. James Moroka, the courtly and old-fashioned president of the African National Congress. Dr. Moroka needed to approve a letter of protest that Mandela had drafted to send to the South African president. On the way there, in a small village in the Free State, one of the most conservative areas of South Africa, Mandela's car grazed a white boy on a bicycle. The boy was shaken up but not hurt. The first thing Mandela did was to duck down and hide a copy of *New Age*, a newspaper that was a favorite of ANC members, which had been sitting on the front seat of the car. Just owning a copy of a banned publication in those days could yield a five-year prison sentence. A police sergeant arrived a few moments later, took a look at him and the injured boy, and said, *"Kaffer, jy sal kak vandag!"* (Kaffir, you will shit today!) Mandela replied, "I don't need a policeman to tell me where to shit." He paused when telling the story, and then said, "I decided to be aggressive, but I was frightened. I can pretend that I'm brave and that I can beat the whole world . . ." And then his voice trailed off.

I can pretend that I'm brave. In fact, that is what he did. And that is how he would describe courage: pretending to be brave. Fearlessness is stupidity. Courage is not letting the fear defeat you. When the policeman advanced on him, Mandela told him to be careful, that he was a lawyer and he could ruin the policeman's career. Then, as Mandela writes in his Robben Island diary, "No one could have been more surprised than myself when I noticed the sergeant hesitate." It had worked. Later than evening, the policeman released him and he was back on his way.

Mandela tells a similar story about his first trip to Robben Island in May 1963. He was being held in jail during the Rivonia Trial—the case that eventually put him away for life. In the middle of the night, he and a few others were told by a sarcastic warder that they were going someplace beautiful—*Die Eiland,* as they say in Afrikaans. Joining Mandela was an older prisoner named Steve Tefu, a member of the Communist Party, who had a temper. Mandela recalls that when they arrived at the Island, they were herded like cattle. Mandela and Tefu were lagging, and as Mandela recalls, a guard said, "Look here, we will kill you here, and your parents, your people, will never know what has happened to you. And we are giving you a last warning!" When they reached the main holding cell, the guards shouted, *"Trek uit! Trek uit!"* ("undress" in Afrikaans).

When the prisoners were naked, the guards started harassing one in particular. Mandela recalls: "The captain says, 'Now why is your hair long?' to one of us. Now he chose a chap, you know, who was very gentle, a gentleman who didn't want to quarrel with anybody, wouldn't hurt a fly, and he was finding it difficult to answer. So this captain says, 'I'm talking to you! You know the regulations! Your hair should have been cut off! Why did you leave your hair like this boy,' " he says, then pointing directly at Mandela. Mandela continues: "So I say to him, 'Now look here . . .' Oh, it was enough! I couldn't continue with the sentence. He says, 'Never talk to me like that!' and he was now advancing."

Mandela paused here and then leaned forward in his chair. His eyes had a faraway look. "It was clear that he was going to assault me and I must confess . . . I must confess I was afraid. You cannot defend yourself, can't fight back."

And yet he did. He told me, "I said to the captain, 'You dare touch me, and I will take you to the highest court in the land and by the time I'm finished with you, you will be as poor as a church mouse.' Well, he stopped . . . I was frightened. It was not because I was courageous, but one had to put up a front."

One had to put up a front. Sometimes it is only through putting up a brave front that you discover true courage. Sometimes the front *is* your courage.

In prison, courage was demonstrated one day at a time. It was not just on the occasions when one had to publicly stand up to a guard, it was simply in walking tall, maintaining your daily dignity, your sense of optimism and hope. One day in 1969, a warder came to Mandela's cell with devastating news: Mandela's oldest son, Thembi, had been killed in a car crash. It was one of the few times during all those years that Mandela did not leave his cell during the day. Walter Sisulu, his oldest friend, was the only one who visited him, and they sat in silence, holding hands.

The next day, Mandela went to the lime quarry to work like all the other prisoners. When I asked him about his son's death, he said it was something almost too much to bear, but he had to show both the guards and his fellow prisoners that he was not disabled by it. Once again, he put up a front. He felt he had no other option.

We think of others being nervous about meeting Mandela, but he was often nervous about meeting others. He was especially anxious the first time he met the South African state president, P. W. Botha. Botha was known as *Die Groot Krokodil,* The Big Crocodile, because of his harsh and blustery manner and his autocratic way of governing. Mandela was then in the last years of his sentence, and it would be the first time an imprisoned member of the ANC would meet the South African state president. In his mind, he rehearsed what he would say and what he would do. He would, if he could, take the initiative. For that very reason, he deliberately strode across the room, greeting Botha with a robust handshake and a wide smile. He disarmed the South African president with his own friendliness and informal manner, something that he had planned and practiced. He put up a front.

In early 1980, not long before Mandela was transferred off Robben Island, a prisoner took a copy of the collected works of Shakespeare to all the political prisoners in Cell Block C and asked them to mark their favorite passages. Mandela did not hesitate. He turned to *Julius Caesar*, act 2, scene 2, and circled this passage:

> *Cowards die many times before their deaths*
> *The valiant never taste of death but once.*
> *Of all the wonders I yet have seen*
> *It seems to me most strange that men fear,*
> *Seeing that death, a necessary end*
> *Will come when it will come.*

A coward might select that passage to give the impression that he was courageous, but for Mandela the passage is not bravado, but a simple statement of reality. Pretend to be brave and you not only become brave, you *are* brave.

Mandela does not see bravery as the province of only a few. Some are tested greatly, but everyone is tested somehow. He always said to me that his wife Winnie had been far braver than he, even though he had been in prison for longer than she had. While he was sealed off from life's daily problems, he explained, she had to wrestle with the daily difficulties of life under apartheid and raise two girls.

Mandela's highest praise for someone he considers

courageous is, "He did very well." By that he does not mean that the fellow was a dramatic hero or that he risked his life in a great endeavor, but that, day in and day out, he remained steady under trying circumstances. That, day in and day out, he resisted giving in to fear and anxiety. All of us are capable of that kind of bravery—and, fortunately, that is the only bravery most of us are called on to demonstrate.

2

Be Measured

I WAS ONCE SITTING NEXT to Mandela in the back-seat of his armor-plated BMW, and his driver was lost. This was not unusual—his motorcade often went awry. The driver was accelerating and making screeching turns as if to make up for lost time. Mandela leaned forward and said to the fellow, "Let's be calm, man."

Let's be calm. In the midst of turbulent situations, Mandela is calm and looks for calm in others. In fact, he radiates calm. Lose control and you lose the situation. Ahmed Kathrada was in prison with Mandela for nearly three decades and says he only saw him angry on two occasions—and both involved warders insulting Winnie. Yes, there may be times that call for an outburst or an impassioned response, but Mandela would say they are very rare, and that they should be calculated, not spontaneous. Control is the measure of a leader—indeed, of all human beings. Calm, he always says, is what people look for in tense situations, whether political or personal. They want to see that you are not rattled, that you are weighing all the factors, and that your response is measured.

In 1993, South Africa was at a knife edge. While Mandela was continuing his negotiations with the government over a new constitution and the date of a democratic election, there were forces within the country trying to undermine this new dispensation, including extreme right-wing military groups that were marshaling their strength and threatening violence. Within his own movement, the African National Congress, some were questioning Mandela's authority, suggesting that he was too conservative, too trusting of the government, and that young leaders like Chris Hani, the head of the ANC's military wing, should be vaulted forward.

Hani was then the second most popular leader in South Africa after Mandela. Always clad in fatigues and a rakishly tilted beret, Hani cut a dynamic figure. He seemed the opposite of Mandela: Where Mandela said forgive and forget, Hani said remember and retaliate; where Mandela spoke in muted tones, Hani shouted; where Mandela talked about keeping the traditional white economy going, Hani, a committed Communist, urged redistributing the wealth to the people. There were those in the ANC who thought Hani, then a youthful fifty-one, was the future of the party and South Africa, rather than Mandela. It seemed to be Hani's moment. South Africa was in grave danger of a full-on civil war between white and black. The white right wing was arming for a fight and there were those on the left, like Hani, who were urging people to prepare for battle. The nightmare of a national race war seemed on the verge of becoming a reality.

In April of that year, I went with Mandela to his house in the Transkei, the rural part of South Africa where he grew up. Mandela's house in the Transkei is within sight of the valley where he was born. "Every man," he once said to me, "should have a house near where he was born." The house itself was then an unpretentious, L-shaped one-story building. It sits in the rolling green and rocky hills—the veldt, as South Africans call it—that he used to play in as a boy. What many people find curious about the house is that it is modeled on the building he stayed in at Victor Verster prison, which was his last address before being released in 1990. I once asked him about this and he smiled. He said he had liked that house very much, and when he knew he was going to build a home for himself in the Transkei, he asked the prison services for a floor plan and a blueprint.

The house itself is set back from the main road and not within sight of any other homes. It has a modest gate and a winding driveway. Even though it is relatively remote and the home of a renowned, historical figure, people from nearby villages—women draped in blankets, old men with walking sticks—wander over and sit or stand in the front yard, either waiting to pay their respects or be fed, or both. It is the local custom and has been the same for hundreds of years. No one makes appointments; people just appear.

Mandela flourished in the Transkei—he seemed less weighed down and more rested. He has always referred to himself as a country boy, which some find a little disingenuous, but when you see him in the country, you can still see a glimmer of that boy. He enjoyed talking to the locals—people who had probably never ventured more than ten miles in any direction from where they lived. He laughed more; he told jokes in his native language of Xhosa; he dandled small children on his knee. Most of the people lived very much as Mandela himself had more than half a century before.

The other thing he enjoyed when he was in the Transkei was early morning walks in the countryside. Mandela would routinely wake up at about four-thirty A.M. and he would emerge for his walk between five and five-thirty. He would generally walk for three to four hours, returning between nine and ten. I had been down to the Transkei with him once before, in December. As often as I could, I would accompany him on his morning constitutional.

One morning that spring—it was April 10—I arrived at his house at five minutes to five. It was still dark. A couple of his bodyguards were sitting in a car listening to music. It was unseasonably cold and I could see them blowing on their hands through the foggy windows. Mandela emerged from his house a little after five, wearing his favorite black-and-gold tracksuit. He started walking south.

Each morning, he would choose a different route, hoping to see some sights from his boyhood or stumble upon a village he had not visited before. He liked to point out landmarks and explain their history. That morning, as always, we were accompanied by his bodyguards. Usually, two walked in front of him and two behind. I would walk about ten feet to the side, close enough to hear him if he wanted to talk, far enough away that he could feel alone. Walks for him were a kind of meditation, and we usually walked in silence.

After more than an hour, we came to a few small *rondavels* on the side of the hill. Rondavels are the round stucco huts with pointed thatched roofs in which Mandela grew up and the people of this area still live. The walls are still made smooth with cow dung and the floors are dried mud. A woman about Mandela's age emerged from one of the rondavels and regarded us skeptically. (Very often, people did not recognize Mandela and thought he was a local chief who had come to visit.) The woman put her hands on her hips and then asked Mandela in Xhosa if he and the rest of us had come by foot. Mandela said yes. She looked down at Mandela's feet and said, "Then why aren't your shoes wet with the morning dew?" Mandela looked down at his shoes, which were dry, and then burst out laughing. This is what he would call the wisdom of the countryside.

By eight, the sun was already powerful and it felt very warm. Mandela always seemed to get stronger as we walked. He would start slowly and then his strides would grow longer and firmer. It was the reverse for the rest of us—all of whom were decades younger. We had been walking in a long, lazy circle, and nearly four hours later, when we were near his house, he pointed to the crest of a hill overlooking Qunu, his ancestral village, where we saw the crumbling remains of a white brick building.

"That was my first school," he said.

He said it had been a one-room schoolhouse, with small windows on either side and a smooth mud floor. It had a tin roof that made a rat-tat-tat clatter when it rained. This was where his first teacher, Miss Mdingane, had given him the name Nelson. In those days, every child in the school was given an English name.

He walked to the hill behind the school and pointed to a large round stone, about seventy-five feet in diameter. They would find a smooth flat stone about the size of tea saucer, sit on it, and ride it down the face of the larger rock. He said he used to rip the seats of his pants that way. "I would get a hiding from my mother for ruining my school clothes," he said.

More than four hours after we started, we trudged back to the house. There were half a dozen people milling around the front, and when we entered the living room, there were eight or ten people sitting inside. Ever the amiable host, Mandela greeted them while I went to the study to set up for our session. When he came in a few minutes later, I asked them who they were. He replied that Miriam, the housekeeper, said they had come to the door and were hungry. Mandela treated them as though they were visiting dignitaries.

Miriam was getting our breakfast ready and Mandela said, "Let's begin." About twenty minutes later—still without breakfast—one of the bodyguards started lurking around the door. "Do you want something?" Mandela said. The guard explained in Xhosa that the East London rugby team was in the front yard. "Ah,"

Mandela said. The day before, he had promised a colleague that he would say hello to the East London rugby team that was visiting the area. "Yes, I remember," Mandela said, and unhooked his microphone with a gesture of mild annoyance.

One of the things I had discovered about him was that even though he was a stickler for punctuality, he would interrupt whatever he was doing for these impromptu greetings or meetings. I don't think he relished them, but he realized that he would save time by doing things as they happened. He sometimes jokingly called this "African time," implying that others around him did not have the respect for punctuality that he did.

Standing and shuffling their feet outside in the driveway were about twenty-five burly black men in green and yellow rugby jerseys. He began to say hello to each one, shaking each man's hand and asking a few rapid-fire questions. About ten minutes into his greeting, he was summoned inside to take a call from one of his closest aides. He took the call in the kitchen, which was a mess of plates and unwashed pots and pans. As he listened, still as a statue, his face became drawn and concerned. When he is concerned, his lips turn downward into a stern frown. Finally he said, "Thank you," and put the phone down.

"Chris Hani has been shot and killed," he said. I

asked by whom. He said he did not know, and then with an icy look, he strode out of the kitchen and back to the driveway to continue shaking hands with the East London rugby team.

The country was at a terrible tipping point, and Hani's assassination could pitch it into civil war. Hani's millions of supporters could easily call out for vengeance and trigger a war between black and white. This was something Mandela wanted to avoid at all costs—but at that moment, he had decided that the proper thing to do was to finish his business with the East London rugby team.

I watched through the window as Mandela smiled and joked and finished greeting the rugby team. He said nothing to them about what had happened. Moments later, a grim-faced Mandela returned to the study. He sat down and the first thing he said was, "Can you see if they are bringing the porridge?" I went into the kitchen, and when our breakfast came, we ate in silence. Mandela was deep in thought.

When he finished his cereal, he asked for his diary and then made a rapid series of phone calls to his closest colleagues: arranging for his immediate return to Johannesburg, asking for details on the police investigation, suggesting that he should go on national television that evening to discuss the murder—all in stern but even tones, with brief, sharp questions and answers. When he was done, he stood up and politely apologized to me for having to cut short our session, and walked out of the room.

In the days after the assassination, there were press reports and stories circulated even within the ANC that Mandela had been "broken up" and "frantic" about Hani's death. In fact, he was icily calm and analytical, reckoning with plans for the immediate future and the consequences of the murder. In the moments that I have been with Mandela in a crisis, he has always been intensely calm, entering a kind of Zen state that seems to slow down the events swirling around him.

Mandela and not F. W. de Klerk, the state president, went on national television that night to discuss the assassination. It was he and not the state president who sought to address the nation's hopes and fears, and not just the concerns of his own party or constituents. De Klerk issued a press release. In the hours after the murder, the police had revealed that the killer was a white Polish immigrant to South Africa and that he had been caught because an Afrikaans woman had memorized his license plate and reported it to the police. That night, Mandela wore a somber expression as he began his speech:

Tonight I am reaching out to every single South African, black and white, from the very depths of my being. A white man, full of prejudice and hate, came to our country and committed a deed so foul that our whole nation now teeters on the brink of disaster. A white woman, of Afrikaner origin, risked her life so that we may know, and bring to justice, this assassin. The cold-blooded murder of Chris Hani has sent shock waves throughout the country and the world. Our grief and anger is tearing us apart. What has happened is a national tragedy that has touched millions of people across the political and colour divide.

He ended the speech this way:

This is a watershed moment for all of us. Our decisions and actions will determine whether we use our pain, our grief, and our outrage to move forward to what is the only lasting solution for our country—an elected government of the people, by the people, and for the people.

He used the word *discipline* four times in his brief speech, noting that Hani was a soldier and a man of "iron discipline," and that South Africans must also act with discipline to honor his memory. *Discipline* was a watchword for him—and through the Hani crisis, he maintained a rigid discipline regarding what he said and thought. In that moment, months before the first democratic election in South African history, he became the as yet unelected leader of white and black South Africans.

As he would confide to me years later, after he had become the president of South Africa, he believed that those first few days after Hani's assassination were the moment that a free and democratic South Africa was most in jeopardy, the moment when he believed the nation that he so loved was closest to a race war of black against white on a scale never seen before. His measured response to this crisis was a large part of the reason that South Africa did not plunge into civil war.

\# \# \#

Sometimes being calm comes perilously close to being dull, but this does not seem to bother Mandela. He would always prefer to err on the side of being calm and dull than being exciting and excitable. He likes to tell the story of a letter he received from a woman in Cape Town who had attended that first famous rally outside City Hall after his release. The woman said that she was glad that he had been released from prison and that she wanted him to succeed in uniting South Africa, but that his speech was "very boring." He always laughs deeply when telling this story. Indeed, no one would confuse the post-prison Nelson Mandela with a great orator. In fact, he would often don clunky glasses to read long speeches in a relentless monotone. One day I asked him, "Seriously though, people do sometimes criticize your speeches for being a bit dull. What do you say to that?"

"You know, I try not to be a rabble-rouser," he said. "The people want to see how you handle situations. They want things explained to them clearly and rationally. I have mellowed. I was very radical as a young man, fighting everybody, using high-flown language."

Yes, as a young man he often tried to create a stir, but the idea for him now is that it is better to be a little dull and trustworthy than fiery and unclear. His remarks are anti–sound bites; he wants his answers to be clear and full and explanatory. He believes that people are willing to tolerate a little dullness in exchange for reliability and substance.

At times his deliberate style could even be a tactic, a kind of jujitsu. Ahmed Kathrada once told me that in prison Mandela enjoyed playing draughts—what Americans call checkers—and that he was the draughts champion of Robben Island. Part of Mandela's strategy, Kathrada said, was to psychologically undermine his opponents through his style of play. He always took a great deal of time between moves, pondering the possibilities. Sometimes he would take extra time if he thought it would annoy or rattle his opponent.

One of his regular opponents was a prisoner named Don Davis, who often challenged Mandela to matches. He was determined that he, and not Mandela, would be the champion of the Island. I once asked Mandela about Davis, and he described him as a "colorful fellow" who had been very brave in resisting the authorities. But what made him militant in resisting the authorities, Mandela noted, did not make him a master of draughts.

"He didn't have the temperament of a sportsman, and when it came to competitions, his whole temperament would change," Mandela once told me with a broad smile. "He would be extra-aggressive. When I played, you see, I was always very steady. That destroyed many opponents, and he was most vulnerable to this tactic."

We think of temperament as something we're born with. But in Mandela's case, it was something he formed.

As a young man, he was hot-headed and easily roused to anger. The man who emerged from prison was the opposite and almost impossible to rile. He waited before making decisions. He considered all options. It is impossible to have perfect knowledge of every situation before making a decision, and we would paralyze ourselves if we insisted on it. But Mandela's example shows the value of forming as complete a picture as possible before taking action. Most of the mistakes he has made in his life came from acting too hastily rather than too slowly. Don't hurry, he would say; think, analyze, then act.

3

Lead from the Front

THROUGHOUT HIS LIFE, Mandela took risks to lead. If he were a soldier, he would be the one jumping out of the foxhole and leading the charge across the field of battle. His view is that leaders must not only lead, they must be *seen* to be leading—that is part of the job description. It is almost as though he is afraid that anyone would ever say or think that he was unwilling to take those risks. Even in personal relationships, he believed that you should take the lead. If there is something bothering you, if you feel you have been treated unfairly, you must say so. That is leading too.

Leading from the front meant many things. Sometimes he took the words literally, as when he first came onto Robben Island: He stepped to the front of the line of prisoners entering the island, under the stares and taunts of the guards, in order to show the others how to react. Right from the start you had to stand up to the guards, he told his colleagues, and he took the lead in doing so.

But leading from the front also meant doing things that did not necessarily attract attention. It meant not accepting any special preferences and doing the same tasks as other prisoners—like cleaning the warder's chamber pots, or those of his fellow prisoners. There is nothing beneath a leader. Eddie Daniels recalls when he first came onto the Island in the early sixties, Mandela strode across the courtyard to introduce himself. Daniels was in awe of Mandela, and talked about how just watching Mandela was inspiring.

"This was the beauty of Nelson. Just the way he walked. The way he carried himself. It lifted up the other prisoners. It lifted me up. Just to see him walk confidently." Simply in the way Mandela walked he was leading from the front.

Danny, as everyone called him, recalls that once he was ill and did not have the strength to clean his chamber pot. Mandela walked by his cell and "he bent down and took my balie, and then walked to the bathroom to clean it. One's not keen on cleaning someone else's mess. Next morning, Nelson came along. He was the leader of the biggest organization in prison. He could instruct anyone to help me. He came in that morning, and he had his balie under his arm. He said, 'How are you Danny?' He came in and took my balie."

Of course, leading from the front also meant seizing the initiative, and at critical junctures throughout his life, Mandela did. He led the ANC Youth League, he was volunteer in chief in the Defiance Campaign of 1952, he led the decision to turn to the armed struggle, and he dared the government to hang him in the Rivonia Trial of 1963–64. In the trial that sent him to prison for life, he pleaded not guilty—but, he said, he was guilty of fighting for human rights and liberty, guilty of fighting unjust laws, guilty of fighting for his own oppressed people. He admitted to planning an attempted sabotage of the government. He knew he risked receiving the death penalty and did not shy away from that. In his final testimony at trial, he spoke for four hours, ending with these words—the last words he would speak in public until he was finally released from prison in 1990:

> During my lifetime I have dedicated myself to this struggle of the African people. I have fought against white domination, and I have fought against black domination. I have cherished the ideal of a democratic and free society in which all persons live together in

harmony and with equal opportunities. It is an ideal which I hope to live for and to achieve. But if needs be, it is an ideal for which I am prepared to die.

There was silence in the courtroom when he finished. They were the words of a man who knew that they might be his last.

But nothing Mandela ever did had quite the risks and dangers of the secret talks he initiated with the white government in 1985 while he was still in prison. It violated every principle of his movement and his own public statements over the decades. He could have been branded a traitor and become a pariah in his own movement, and he might well have pushed the country to all-out civil war. But he knew that he had to take action. His attitude was, when faced with the inevitable, why wait? That momentous change may have seemed sudden from the outside, but like so many such decisions in his life, it had a long and winding history.

✳ ✳ ✳

It began at Pollsmoor Prison, where Mandela was taken in 1982, after eighteen years on Robben Island. Pollsmoor is perched on the edge of a trim and pleasant Cape Town suburb, below the Steenberg Mountains that begin just north of the whitewashed prison walls. To get to the prison, you drive through the town's one-lane roads, past prim little houses with bicycles on their front lawns. Then, at the end of one unmarked residential street, you turn right and there before you stands the elaborate gate to Pollsmoor Maximum Security Prison.

Insofar as a prison can seem pleasant, Pollsmoor did. The long drive boasts manicured gardens and flower-beds that take you up to the low, light gray concrete building. At Pollsmoor, Mandela missed the natural beauty of Robben Island and the chance to be outside under the sun, but there were consolations. His family could visit more easily. The food was better. They were finally on the mainland and he felt more connected to the world. He and his four close colleagues from the Island—Walter Sisulu, Ahmed Kathrada, Raymond Mhlaba, and Andrew Mlangeni—shared a very large cell, about the size of a high school basketball gym, on the third floor. And there was a spacious deck outside their cell where Mandela was permitted to plant a garden.

By 1985, Mandela had been imprisoned for twenty-two years, and the anti-apartheid movement within South Africa had become more intense and strident. The ANC's campaign to make South Africa "ungovernable" was turning the townships into a war zone. The daily uprisings there were leading evening news broadcasts around the world. The union movement and the United Democratic Front, an umbrella organization for hundreds of anti-apartheid organizations, were putting constant pressure on the government. And Mandela's name and image had become the symbol of the worldwide anti-apartheid movement.

In that same year, Mandela was diagnosed with an enlarged prostate and his doctors recommended surgery. Under extremely tight security, he was taken to Volks Hospital in Cape Town for the procedure. On those few occasions when Mandela needed to go to the mainland when he was on Robben Island, he detested it. He was treated no differently from every other black prisoner. He once told me of being kept in the hold of a boat used by white South Africans to go to the Island and that the passengers had spit on him from above. For all the indignities of Robben Island, they often didn't compare to the humiliations he weathered outside of it.

But this time was different. His stature had changed. He was given a separate wing of the hospital and a sunny room decorated with flowers. The nurses all regarded

him with hushed respect. The operation was successful and he recuperated for several days before being
taken back to Pollsmoor. At the exit of the hospital, he
was picked up in a sedan by the commanding officer
of the prison. This was highly unusual; in the past he
had been transported by ordinary warders in a van.
As they drove back, the officer told him that he would
not be rejoining his colleagues, but that he would be
taken to a different room. Mandela asked him why;
the officer just shrugged and said, Instructions from
Pretoria.

Mandela's new cell was on the ground floor of the
prison and consisted of three dark, dank rooms. It was
palatial by Robben Island standards, but he was discon-
certed by the change. He considered his new situation
from every angle. Why had he been separated from his
colleagues? Why had the commanding officer picked
him up at the hospital? What was the government's
strategy? Normally, he might have lodged a protest or
made some official inquiry, but something told him he
needed to think about it more.

As he began to consider his situation, he thought
not about the deprivations of his new surroundings but
the opportunities. His solitude, he concluded, would
give him a chance to do something that he had been
thinking about for years, something he had made very

tentative inquiries about, something that was heresy from the point of view of the ANC. He could begin talks with the government. For decades, the ANC had refused to negotiate with the government until it agreed to lift apartheid laws and free political prisoners. But now he realized that the world had changed and he needed to change with it. He had long since concluded that the ANC was not going to topple the government through armed struggle. Only negotiations could work. Now he could act on that belief.

In a cell with his fellow prisoners, nothing he did would be private; he would need to consult with them about an absence or a conversation with the authorities. But he was on his own now. It was clear to him that the government looked at his new circumstances as an opportunity as well.

His decision was a momentous one. He had been fighting against white majority rule his entire life. The ANC had been fighting against it for seventy-five years and been engaged in the armed struggle for two decades. The policy for all that time had been not to negotiate, that negotiations could only take place on the basis of equality. Mandela, without consulting anyone, was going to change the course of all of this history. He would be departing from the avowed strategy of the

ANC, the organization that he loved and that had nourished him and to which he felt the greatest of all possible loyalties.

He was wary, though, and had good reason to be. This was not the first time that the idea of talks had come up. Earlier that year, in January, the South African president, P. W. Botha, had publicly offered to release Mandela if he unconditionally renounced violence as a political instrument. Mandela had rejected the offer out of hand, releasing a statement that said, "Only free men can negotiate. Prisoners cannot enter into contracts. I cannot and will not give any undertaking at a time when I and you, the people, are not free. Your freedom and mine cannot be separated." Mandela's blunt and militant response embarrassed the government and President Botha.

But this time it felt different. He would be starting the talks confidentially and on his own initiative. The anti-apartheid movement was growing in power. The government was beginning to see the writing on the wall. Botha had told his countrymen that they had to "adapt or die." At the same time, Mandela knew the status quo could go on for decades, and he was not getting any younger. He also knew that he could not be seen by his colleagues, his party, or the world as commencing negotiations. What he did was write a confidential letter to Kobie Coetsee, the minister of justice, saying that he would like to begin talks with the government.

Progress was glacial. From the moment he wrote his first letter to the time of the first meeting took almost two years. He did not know if the government was considering his offer or not, and he kept writing letters. But in July 1986, things suddenly went into overdrive.

"I still remember very well," he recalled. "It was a Wednesday when I gave them the letter, merely saying to the commissioner, 'I want to see you on a matter of major national importance.'" The following Sunday, Mandela was summoned to the commissioner's house, which was on the grounds of the prison. When Mandela was face-to-face with the commissioner, he said what he really wanted was to see the minister of justice. The commissioner asked him why.

"I want to raise the whole question of talks between the ANC and the government," Mandela said. The commissioner immediately phoned Coetsee, who was in Cape Town. Coetsee, according to Mandela, said, "Bring him over to my house right now." Mandela never returned to his cell but was taken to Coetsee's official residence in Cape Town in his dusty prison overalls, where he spent the next three hours.

Mandela never liked to meet with people unless he

was on an equal footing. He did not like the fact that he was still in his prison uniform, but he let that pass.

"Now I said to him, I want to see P. W. Botha, the state president," he recalled. Mandela had demanded a meeting with the minister of justice only to tell him that what he really wanted was a meeting with the state president. Mandela was using each man to take things up to the next level. Mandela's request to Coetsee had ratcheted up the negotiations to the highest level—a secret meeting between the world's most famous political prisoner and the man who ultimately kept him behind bars. Coetsee realized immediately how historic this session was. That day began a chain of events that culminated not just in Mandela's release, but also in the negotiations that led to the first free and democratic election in South Africa's history.

✳   ✳   ✳

When you lead from the front, you can't let your colleagues get too far behind. So after these private talks had begun, Mandela made a request to see his comrades. He wanted to tell them what he had done and to make sure they were with him. Even though they were just three floors apart, the request to see them had to go to the prison authorities, then to the bureaucracy in Cape

Town, and finally to government headquarters in Pretoria. This time the authorities would only permit him to see his colleagues individually. Instead of resisting, Mandela agreed. His first meeting was with Walter, his oldest friend and colleague, his mentor, the man who had first seen a mass leader in that rough and gangly youth from the Transkei. He told Walter of the secret negotiations.

Mandela recalled for me Walter's reaction, which was not positive. "He said, 'Well, I am not in principle against negotiations, but I would have wished for them to start by them, not by us.' I said to him, 'If you are not against negotiations in principle, then it doesn't matter who starts. *I have started.*' "

Mandela in turn saw Mhlaba, Kathrada, and Mlangeni. Kathrada agreed with Walter and was against the negotiations. Mhlaba and Mlangeni reacted the same way: What had he been waiting for?

But that was not the reaction of the ANC leadership based in Lusaka, Zambia. In fact, when his close friend Oliver Tambo, the head of the ANC, heard rumors that Mandela was talking to the government, he was gravely concerned. There were those who thought Mandela had been broken or had sold out. Tambo sent him a letter asking him to explain.

"So I said to him," Mandela recalled, "Comrade

O.R.—that's what I used to call him—I am discussing with the government, one thing, one thing only, a meeting between the ANC and the government. That is all. Full stop."

In deciding to begin negotiations, he well knew that it was at risk to his own leadership. Besides Tambo, there were those within the ANC—some at very high levels— who felt he had betrayed the movement. Some even called him a traitor. There is no doubt that this jeopardized his anointed role as the ultimate leader of the ANC and the head of the anti-apartheid movement. There were already those within the ANC who were plotting against him and this gave them ammunition.

Mandela had said to me many times that the ANC was a collective in which no one person was the ultimate decider. So I asked him about this transformational decision he had effectively made on his own.

Mandela was quite direct. "It is absolutely necessary at times for the leader to take on independent action without consulting anybody and to present what he has done to the organization. There are cases of that nature where I will take a decision and confront you with it, and the only question that you have to consider is whether what I have done is in the interest of the movement. I say if I had discussed the question [of negotiations] with my colleagues before I went to see the government, they would have turned it down. We would not have been having negotiations today."

For Mandela, leading from the front also means being accountable. He embraces the idea that if he makes a decision on his own, he will bear the consequences for it. If he's wrong, he says, you know who to blame. To this day, he regards the decision to negotiate with Botha as perhaps the most revolutionary he ever made. Once he decided that there could be no military victory but only a negotiated settlement, he did not hesitate to change course.

✳   ✳   ✳

In his life, Mandela has often changed his mind when circumstances change. To him, that is simple common sense. When he sees what he regards as the inevitable, he will alter his point of view. But he does not turn on a dime. He likes to examine all the consequences of reversing himself. Only then will he act. To the outside, his actions can sometimes seem precipitous—but inside, he will have already thought it through. He would say don't postpone the inevitable even though it might not be the solution you originally wanted.

During the time we were working together, I went with him on a trip to Washington, D.C. At a press conference there, he said that it had become time for America and the world to end sanctions against South Africa. This change in policy came as a surprise to many of Mandela's colleagues in the ANC and outside. It is something they had been discussing for months, but had been deadlocked about. Sometimes, he would say, you just have to break the logjam. He had searched for consensus but could not reach it. He prefers consensus, but if it is impossible, he will take the initiative on his own. In the case of sanctions, he had talked to me about the idea and said he was thinking about it—which usually meant he had already decided and was testing the waters.

When he left office in 1999, he vowed that he would go into a quiet retirement. But it was not to be. He could not remain silent in the face of what AIDS was doing to South Africa. He knew very little about the disease when he emerged from prison. In fact, he still had some unreconstructed views of AIDS and homosexuality that were consistent with a man of his generation. But after he left office and watched his successor, Thabo Mbeki, mishandle South Africa's AIDS crisis, he spoke out. Mbeki long denied the connection between the HIV virus and AIDS and refused to allow the universal distribution of antiretroviral drugs to South African AIDS patients.

Finally, in 2002, Mandela told the Johannesburg *Sunday Times*, "This is a war. It has killed more people than has been the case in all previous wars and in all previous natural disasters. We must not continue to be debating, to be arguing, when people are dying." Mbeki wasn't happy about what Mandela had said, but it was the right thing to do. Sometimes leading from the front is admitting you have been wrong—even when no one else is accusing you of being wrong. Mandela realized he had been slow to see the light, and he could not help but try to correct the record.

Even from the sidelines, Mandela was leading from the front.

4

Lead from the Back

AS MUCH AS MANDELA LOVED the limelight, he always knew he had to share it. He understood that some part—quite a large part—of leadership is symbolic and that he was a splendid symbol. But he knew that he could not always be in front, and that his own great goal could die unless he empowered others to lead. In the language of basketball, he wanted the ball, but he understood that he had to pass to others and let them shoot. Mandela genuinely believed in the virtues of the team, and he knew that to get the best out of his own people, he had to make sure that they partook of the glory and, even more important, that they felt they were influencing his decisions.

One morning, we had been walking for about an hour and a half in the hills behind his house in the Transkei, and the early mist had cleared. It was an area strewn with rocks and boulders, with dry, short grass and few trees. Mandela stopped, lifted his head, and looked

around. He said this area used to be a mealie field—
mealie being the African term for corn.

"It was lovely. We were supposed to be watching the
cattle, but we would sometimes steal some mealies and
roast them. We would look for large anthills that had
been abandoned. All that was left inside were some
dried pieces of grass and a few termites. We would take
the corn and put it in the old ant hole and light a fire
with the dried grass at the bottom. Then we would place
the cob in the hole and the corn would roast while the
termites provided a kind of oil that made the corn very
tasty." It was as though he were transported back to his
boyhood and was tasting the charred corn as he was
talking.

He turned to me and said, "You have never herded
cattle, have you, Richard?" I said I had not. He nodded.
As a young boy—as early as eight or nine years old—
Mandela had spent long afternoons herding cattle. His
mother owned some cattle of her own, but there was a
collective herd belonging to the village that he and other
boys would look after. He then explained to me the
rudiments of herding cattle.

"You know, when you want to get the cattle to move
in a certain direction, you stand at the back with a stick,
and then you get a few of the cleverer cattle to go to the
front and move in the direction that you want them to

go. The rest of the cattle follow the few more-energetic cattle in the front, but you are really guiding them from the back."

He paused. "That is how a leader should do his work."

The story is a parable, but the idea is that leadership at its most fundamental is about moving people in a certain direction—usually through changing the direction of their thinking and their actions. And the way to do that is not necessarily by charging out front and saying, "Follow me," but by empowering or pushing others to move forward ahead of you. It is through empowering others that we impart our own leadership or ideas. It is valuable in every arena of life. We see it in the workplace when a manager encourages her employees to help formulate new strategies. We see it at home when parents have a family meeting to guide their children toward sensible rules and behavior, rather than simply laying down the law.

One of Mandela's longtime colleagues once said to me that because Mandela was so strong and charismatic, he never got credit for just how clever he was. People often remarked on his presence, not his intelligence. But while Mandela would not underestimate his own bandwidth, he knew he was not a quick study. He had to work at it.

He always put in the hours because he wanted to truly understand things and examine issues from all sides. He was never facile enough that he could feign knowledge that he did not actually possess. As a result, he often aligned himself with those he thought were brighter and quicker than he. He wanted to learn from those he thought had true expertise, and he was never shy about asking them to explain things for him. And by asking for their help or counsel, he would not only learn from them but also empower them and make them allies. Mandela understood that there is nothing that ingratiates you with someone else as much as asking for his help—that when you defer to others, you increase their allegiance to you.

⁂　⁂　⁂

Mandela's model for leading from behind was not his father but Jongintaba, the king who raised him in the Great Place. After Mandela's father died, his mother packed up a small satchel of Nelson's belongings and walked through the hills of the Transkei to Mqhekezweni, the capital of Thembuland, known as the Great Place. Mandela's father had been a counselor to the king, and the king wanted to groom Mandela to eventually be a counselor to his own son, Justice, who was Mandela's contemporary. Mandela recalls the long, quiet journey there from Qunu, his home village, walking on foot with his mother. He was sad about leaving the only world he had ever known, but when he got to the Great Place, he was dazzled by its grandeur. As he wrote in his prison diary, "I could hardly imagine anything on earth which could exceed this." In fact, the Great Place wasn't much more than a dozen or so rondavels and a large garden. It was quite modest even by the standards of an African royal court. But he thought he had landed in the center of the world.

On the afternoon he arrived, he recalled a long motorcar gliding through the western gate of the village, and all the men of the village who were sitting in the shade rising to their feet and calling out, *"Bayethe a-a-a Jongintaba!"* (Hail Jongintaba!), the traditional Xhosa salute to the chief. As Mandela remembers it in his diary, "A short thick-set man, dark complexioned and wearing a smart suit, stepped out and joined the gathering under the trees. He had a resolute bearing and an intelligent face. His confidence and casual manner marked him off as one who was used to praise and exercise of authority." It was King Jongintaba.

That day was imprinted on his memory for the rest of his life. As he says in his diary, until arriving in Mqhekezweni, his only ambition was to be a champion stick fighter or a great hunter. "But even on that first day," he writes, "I felt like a tree that had been pulled out root and branch from the earth and flung midstream into a strong current." That current was the path of leadership—but how it would guide him into the larger world was something he could not then imagine.

Mandela closely observed the style and manner of the king. Chieftaincy was the pivot around which the life of the community—and his own life—revolved. The king was not an educated man (he could neither read nor write), but he was the custodian of Thembu history and custom. The king may have been born to leadership, but he was also seen as the people's servant. Chieftaincy was treated as a privilege, not just a right. The chiefly style of leadership was not about vaulting oneself to the front but about listening and achieving consensus.

The meetings of the royal court, which were like democratic town hall meetings, were the locus of leadership. All of the men from the village came, and anyone who wanted to speak could do so. It was the custom for the chief to listen to the views of his counselors and the community before uttering his own opinion. The king always stood up straight and proud, and when he spoke at the end of a meeting he would summarize the views that he had heard. The king was strong willed, but he did not let his own will supersede that of the community.

This is what Mandela means by leading from behind. A good chief does not grandly state his opinion and command others to follow him. He listens, he summarizes, and then he seeks to mold opinion and steer people toward an action, not unlike the young boy herding cattle from the back. Mandela regards this as the best of the African tradition of leadership. He sees the West as the bastion of personal ambition, where people fight to get ahead and leave others behind. The Renaissance idea of individualism never penetrated Africa like it did Europe and America. The African model of leadership is better expressed as *ubuntu,* the idea that people are empowered by other people, that we become our best selves through unselfish interaction with others.

I remember arriving one weekend morning at Mandela's house in Houghton. In the driveway, beyond the front gates, Mandela and a group of his advisers sat in the shade in a small circle of folding chairs, engrossed in discussion. I pulled up a chair just outside the circle. What struck me most forcefully was that these men were talking animatedly, some of them criticizing Mandela and telling him very directly that he was wrong about certain positions. All the men were respectful (a few just barely), and some were quite fiery and outspoken. Mandela sat straight, almost unmoving, listening intently with a neutral expression. He would make an excellent poker player. Only at the end of the meeting, as the fellows were getting ready to go, did Mandela speak, and he summarized their views without saying exactly where he stood. I noticed that the men seemed more jovial once they had gotten their opinions off their chest, regardless of whether or not they had persuaded Mandela. Mandela knew that the surest way to defuse an argument is to listen patiently to the opposing point of view.

I later asked him about this discussion and his leadership style. "We are a democratic organization," he told me. "I sometimes come to the NEC [National Executive Committee] with an idea and they disagree with me and overrule me. And I obey them, even when they are wrong! That is democracy!" He gave a great belly laugh. But he knew that in many instances, his own views on individual issues mattered far less than the democratic process—that it was better to lose on an individual matter and allow democracy to win.

When Mandela became president, he presided over cabinet meetings in the same way. He did his best to see that opposing views were aired, if not always adhered to.

He almost always spoke last, and more briefly than any-one else.

On occasion, he mentioned Abraham Lincoln to me as a model of leadership. He had learned about him as a schoolchild. In fact, as a young man, Mandela had wanted the role of Lincoln in a school play, but there was one student even taller than he was who got the part. (Mandela ruefully acknowledged that he ended up playing John Wilkes Booth.) Mandela was aware that Lincoln had put some of his fiercest rivals in his cabinet—and Mandela likewise put members of the op-position in his own first cabinet. He was impressed by the way Lincoln used persuasion rather than force in managing his cabinet. He once told me an anecdote he recalled about Lincoln talking someone out of being in his cabinet and ended by saying, "It is wise to persuade people to do things and make them think it is their own idea."

For Mandela, leading from the back can in some ways seem like a camouflage for leading from the front. But he also understands the limits of any one person's leadership, even his own. When he emerged from prison, he was a kind of African Rip Van Winkle. Friends and colleagues tutored him on everything under the sun: women's rights, the modern media, AIDS and

HIV, and dozens of other subjects. This was both a necessary remedial education and an expression of the African idea of collective leadership. Since boyhood he had understood that collective leadership was about two things: the greater wisdom of the group compared to the individual, and the greater investment of the group in any result achieved by consensus. It was a double win.

Leading from behind works the same way: You reach the result you want in a harmonious way. It is both good for others and good for you.

5

Look the Part

WE STRIVE TO JUDGE PEOPLE by the content of their character, but Nelson Mandela understood that sometimes the best way to help others see your character is by how you appear. All his life, Mandela was concerned with how things looked—from the color of his shirt to the way a policy appeared to his supporters to how straight he stood. He would never tell anyone not to judge a book by its cover, because he knows we all do. Although he is a man of substance, he would say that it makes no sense *not* to judge by appearances. Appearances matter, and we have only one chance to make a first impression.

Mandela loves clothes. He always has. He would not say that clothes make the man, but they do make an instant impression. His view is that if you want to play the part, you have to wear the right costume. He began to learn this as a small boy when his father cut up a pair of his own riding breeches to make him a pair of trousers for his first day of school. His father was determined that his son not look like an uncivilized "native" wearing a blanket. Later, when he was a young man and had become a ward of the king of Thembuland, one of his chores was to press the king's suits. A king had to look just so, and it was a job Mandela performed with great meticulousness. I remember him once asking me if I could help him find an iron in his hotel room because his jacket was wrinkled. He would note the quality of the cloth of his suits and those other men wore. He recalls with great detail the natty, double-breasted suit the king had made for him before he went off to the University of Fort Hare.

But he was not always able to afford to dress as he wanted to. During his early life in Johannesburg, he owned only one suit over the course of five years, which in the end had more patches than original cloth. He still remembers how embarrassed he was to wear it. A few years later, when he had achieved some success as a young lawyer, one of the first things he did was to find his own tailor. His future lawyer, George Bizos, recalls meeting Mandela in his tailor's offices and noting that it was the first time he had ever seen a black man being fitted for a suit. Mandela had a natural sense of style and in those days was considered something of a dandy. He dressed that way not only because it gave him pleasure, but because in those days, whites judged blacks in part by what they wore, and he did not want to appear as a common laborer but as a professional man.

Actors understand that going to an audition dressed as the character they hope to play can make the difference in getting the part. Just as pretending to be brave can become real courage, we may find that outfitting ourselves as the person we want to be brings us closer to becoming that person. Throughout his life, Mandela always looked—and played—the part. When he was a student, he wanted to look precise and organized. When he was a young lawyer, he wore bespoke suits to impress the judges and his clients. When he went underground, he donned fatigues and grew a beard. When he first became president, he wore conservative dark suits. Later, as South Africa settled down, he abandoned European-style suits and took to wearing custom-made silk shirts in glorious African patterns. They became his sartorial signature; people called them "Mandela shirts." He loves those shirts and has a closet full of them. Beyond his enjoyment of the vivid color, those shirts symbolize a new kind of power—African, indigenous, confident. The shirts are a statement: No longer does an African leader need to dress in a Western style to seem substantial.

✳   ✳   ✳

Given his belief in the symbolic importance of appearances, it is not surprising that one of the first battles Mandela had on Robben Island was over clothing. The regulations said that black prisoners had to wear shorts, whereas prisoners designated as Indian and Colored (mixed race) could wear long pants. He found it insulting that he had to wear short pants like a "garden boy" and fought this as fiercely as any battle he ever waged on the Island. Years later, when he was preparing to meet P. W. Botha for the first time, Mandela felt he should not wear a prison uniform to meet the president of South Africa—that it would put him at a disadvantage. So the prison authorities had a three-piece suit made for him, about which he was very particular. He considered this an essential aspect of putting himself on equal footing with Botha.

When we traveled together, I always wanted to know what he was planning on wearing the following day so that I could dress appropriately. I knew this mattered to him. I would sometimes pop into his room to find out, and he would usually say, "Ah, Richard, I want to know what *you* are going to wear." And he wasn't joking. He would often comment on a suit or tie of mine, and he would sometimes express displeasure if he thought I was underdressed (or overdressed) for a particular occasion.

It helps, of course, that Mandela is tall, slim, and fit. He has beautiful posture. You will never see him hunched over or with his head anything but upright and looking ahead. On Robben Island, he was always aware of how he walked and carried himself. He knew he needed to be seen to be standing up to the authorities, literally and figuratively—even when he was secretly negotiating with them. He understood that people took their cues from him, and if he were confident and unbowed, they would be too.

Long before jogging became a trend, he was a stickler for fitness. He used to run in the early mornings in Johannesburg in the 1950s. Some of this is vanity: He is very proud of his slimness. He is careful about what he eats and he used to cluck a bit at men of his generation who had bellies. When we were together, he often noted who had aged well and who hadn't. Once we were walking in the Transkei and he saw two women of roughly his own age from a nearby village. They commented on how youthful he looked and he beamed. They had not aged so well.

"It is very hard, life in the country, and poverty ages a person," he said. "It is ironical that the program in prison, with its minimal diet and physical activity, promotes long life and youthfulness." Indeed, his prison regimen, with daily physical labor, a spartan diet of grains and vegetables, and its early-to-bed, early-to-rise schedule, resembles that of a spa organized by a gerontologist trying to reverse the aging process. Walter Sisulu used to joke that it was more stressful outside of prison than in, and that he had not had a good night's sleep since leaving jail. Mandela often told me about his morning exercise routine in prison, which included running in place for forty-five minutes followed by two hundred sit-ups and one hundred fingertip push-ups. One day, he popped down on the floor and did two quick fingertip push-ups for me, then dusted his hands off with a satisfied smile.

Mandela was concerned about appearances on a far grander scale than just what suit he was wearing. He understood the power of the image. Long before the Internet and twenty-four-hour cable news, Mandela thought deeply about how his actions would be interpreted by voters or the media, and how his party's policies would appear on the world stage. "Appearances constitute reality," he once said to me. He understood the power of symbols and that they often mattered more than substance. After all, he became the leader of his nation because he united symbol and substance. He was the aristocratic revolutionary, the prisoner without bitterness. From the start, he was the handsome, charismatic figurehead who also understood policy and government. As Walter Sisulu said to me about the moment he first met Mandela in 1941: "We wanted to be a mass movement, and then one day a mass leader walked into my office."

Mandela was a genius at what sociologists call "impression management." Yes, he believed that the African National Congress needed to embrace the armed struggle in order to achieve its aims, but he also believed that some symbolic explosions would unite the anti-apartheid movement behind it. Yes, he wanted to make his case at the famous Rivonia Trial, but he pleaded guilty because he thought it would make him seem more heroic to the outside world. No, he did not actually think his white jailers had been kind to him, but he wanted to show the white public that he was not angry or bitter.

He always did a great deal of planning around how a policy or an action would appear. No detail was too superficial to merit his attention. He analyzed campaign posters and pondered whom he should shake hands with. Many times I sat next to him in the back of his car as he waited for the precise moment to emerge at an event. Whenever he was exiting an airplane or entering a room, he was aware of the figure that he cut and of the exact moment that would earn him maximum attention.

He also understood that being seen to seize the

initiative often confers authority. At any political or social event, he was always the first to stand up and clap, always the first to shake the hands of the performers, always the first to congratulate the winner. He greets people; he is not greeted by them. There is no event at which he will not speak, no matter how small or informal. You cannot stop him from standing up and giving remarks. He is always the host, never the guest. When he first appeared with the Queen of England in London, it was as though he was extending his royal hospitality to a reserved country matron.

One of the impressions he always sought to convey was that he did not play favorites; that he was above any kind of prejudice. On weekends, the authorities allowed the political prisoners to walk to the soccer field to watch the other prisoners play. When he was walking to the field, he would always choose an Indian or a Colored prisoner to walk with to show that he did not believe in grouping people by race. Even in those days, long before he became president, when people asked him what his favorite team was, he would demur.

"I never choose between stars or teams," he said. "It's a tactless thing for a leader to do. I avoid putting any star above the others because you immediately forfeit the support of others. In prison, I would say that I support all of them, that I support the best of them."

Similarly, he was very keen to appear as a man of the people. At events or dinners, he would always walk through the kitchen to shake hands with the staff. At an airport, he would look for the ground crew to shake their hands. As much as he enjoyed the company of celebrities and the famous—and he did—he never wanted to come across as an elitist. He always wanted people to know that he accepted the burdens of leadership as well as its pleasures and that he was accessible to all.

Mandela is a man of incredible discipline, but he also wants to cultivate the *idea* that he is a man of discipline. When we first started working together, I had an appointment with him at his office early on a Saturday morning. When I arrived, just before seven, he was sitting behind his desk in a suit, talking on the phone. It was apparent that he had woken up the person on the other end of the line, who had said something like, "Don't you ever sleep?" And then he said, "Ah, I am an old man, and I can only sleep two hours a night." When he got off the phone, I asked him whether that was true. He laughed and said, "No, I sleep eight hours."

\#   \#   \#

Like Lincoln, who took every opportunity to have his picture taken, Mandela is aware that images have tremendous power to shape how we are perceived. Ever since he was a young man, he has been keen to be photographed. He posed burning his pass card following the Sharpeville uprising; he posed bare-chested in and outside the boxing ring; he posed in his African regalia before the Treason Trial; he even posed for pictures on Robben Island. Long before the existence of blogs and social networking sites, Mandela understood that images endure and that their power to help or hurt you was indelible. All his life, he cultivated and curated images of himself. He helped orchestrate those he wanted to symbolize him and avoided those that would create an impression he did not want.

If you look at old photographs of Mandela, you see something that is rare—even unique—among African men of his generation: a beaming smile. Mandela's smile is among the most radiant in history. It conveys warmth and wisdom, power and generosity, understanding and forgiveness. It was one of the first things that Walter Sisulu noticed about the young man from the Transkei. And this was at a time when Africans were meant to be humble and docile, when a smile on a public figure seemed to suggest a lack of seriousness. Smiles were modern. Mandela's smile spelled confidence. It said he was a happy warrior, not a vengeful one.

Mandela realized early on that his smile was part of

his power. Over the years, being with him on hundreds of occasions when he posed for pictures, I noticed that his smile was fixed and flawless. Like a great actor, he perfected it; you can look at image after image and the smile is identical. It was his mask.

In the election campaign in 1994, his smile *was* the campaign. That smiling iconic campaign poster was everywhere—on billboards, on highways, on street-lamps, at tea shops and fruit stalls. It told black voters that he would be their champion and white voters that he would be their protector. It was the smile of the proverb *"tout comprendre, c'est tout pardonner"*—to under-stand all is to forgive all. It was political Prozac for a nervous electorate.

Ultimately, that was the single most important message he wanted to send after his release: that he was a man without bitterness. His great task as the first democratically elected president of South Africa was to be the father of his country, to unite a heterogeneous battle-scarred land into one nation. From the moment of his release through his entire presidency and beyond, he was intent on showing people that he did not harbor any sense of grievance. From the first press conference where he talked about the generosity of his jailers to the literally hundreds of times he said, "Forget the past," the chief image he conveyed was of the paterfamilias who wanted to forgive and forget. He made appearances with some of his white jailers, including James Gregory, who found his fifteen minutes of fame claiming to be Mandela's friend. Mandela paid a very public visit to the widow of former Prime Minister Hendrik Verwoerd, the father of apartheid. He put his arm around Constand Viljoen, the right-wing former general who had allegedly plotted a coup against him. All of it was in service to this one idea: that he had buried the past; that he was the father of a rainbow nation; that he was looking forward, not backward. He understood that expressing his anger would diminish his power, while hiding it increased it.

But much of this was for show. The private Mandela was deeply pained about what had happened to him. He was aware that he had spent the best years of his life behind bars. He found the views of his jailers and the government leaders to be crabbed and narrow. He did not care for Gregory, whom he found limited and who he thought was exploiting their connection. He fiercely resented the treatment his wife Winnie had received over the decades. He was angered at how his political rivals had sometimes tried to undermine him. He believed that he had sacrificed his marriage and his family to the struggle against oppression and prejudice. But he knew he could never let people see behind the curtain, that he could never expose his true feelings. We live in a far more expressive era than Mandela's, but he would say that one cannot be completely open about one's emotions. Yes, emotions may be authentic, and authenticity is a modern virtue, but one can be authentic without being unnecessarily revealing. That is where his extraordinary discipline came in. And that is why the smile was his mask, disguising any hurt or sadness, hiding as much as it disclosed.

Ultimately, his smile was symbolic of how Mandela molded himself. At every stage of his life he decided who he wanted to be and created the appearance—and then the reality—of that person. He became who he wanted to be.

6

Have a Core Principle—Everything Else Is Tactics

N ELSON MANDELA IS A MAN OF PRINCIPLE— exactly one: Equal rights for all, regardless of race, class, or gender. Pretty much everything else is a tactic.

I know that seems like an exaggeration—but to a degree very few people suspect, Mandela is a thorough-going pragmatist who was willing to compromise, change, adapt, and refine his strategy as long as it got him to the promised land. Almost any means justified that one noble end. In South Africa in the 1980s and 1990s, that meant one thing: the overthrow of apartheid and the achievement of a non-racial democracy with one person, one vote. Full stop.

Mandela has been called a prophet, a saint, a hero. What he is not is a naïve idealist. He is an idealistic pragmatist, even a high-minded one, but at the end of the day, he is about getting things done.

Over and over during the course of our time together, Mandela made a distinction between principles and tactics. (Or principles and strategy—he used the words *tactics* and *strategy* interchangeably.) This view evolved over his time in prison; the man who first went to jail was not nearly as strategic or tactical as the man who came out. As a young man, he was often led by romantic principles and made some decisions he later came to regret. But over his years as a freedom fighter—fighting against an opponent who adhered to few if any principles—and during those long decades in prison, he became the ultimate strategist and tactician.

You would not know this from hearing him speak in public. He talks about noble principles of freedom and democracy, and when he does, his rhetoric sounds pretty much like everyone else's. He knows that a transformational leader does not talk about polls or votes or tactics but about principles and ideas. But when you hear Mandela talk privately about politics, it is a graduate-level course taught by a man whom any presidential candidate would hire as a consultant.

His education in tactics came at great cost, and he learned not only the tactics themselves, but the art of concealing them.

Mandela grew up confident and strong. That was not always the case for a black man in South Africa in the early part of the twentieth century. Colonialism and then apartheid were designed to emasculate black South Africans. From an early age he had an aristocratic bearing. Some of that is in his DNA, but much of it comes from his upbringing in an African royal court. Raised in a nineteenth-century tribal world in which whites barely made an appearance, he was not wounded by discrimination like so many black South Africans of his generation. Whites were a distant presence that did not impinge on his daily life; he did not shake the hand of a white man until he was at boarding school. His world was separate and not equal, but whatever its privations, that separateness allowed him to grow up uninfected by the poison of racism and low expectations. His confidence was a key to his success and was one of the reasons the ANC tapped him as a mass leader.

It was only as he got older, went off to boarding school, and saw class and race differences in action—and especially when he went to Johannesburg, where he was not treated as the son of a chief, but as another poor and ignorant boy from the countryside—that he became fully aware of the chasm between black and white. When he experienced racism and disregard firsthand, it made him angry—angry that he, Nelson Mandela, could be treated that way; angry that anyone could be treated that way; angry enough that he would give up all the more comfortable possibilities in his life to fight that racism. It was his very confidence in himself and his high self-esteem that made him so deeply angry. When people with low self-esteem are treated with low expectations, it confirms their sense of self. When people with high self-esteem are treated the same way, they are offended. Mandela was deeply offended. As a man, Mandela was slow to anger, but when he did become angry, he became profoundly stubborn. In this case, his stubbornness lasted half a century. Although he would vehemently disagree with the notion that all politics is personal, his own politics had its roots in the endless series of personal affronts he experienced as a black man in South Africa.

✽ ✽ ✽

With the support of his patron, King Jongintaba, Nelson Mandela had entered Fort Hare, the only university for blacks in South Africa. It was a tiny, elite institution that had a small campus with Victorian-style buildings clustered around green courtyards. There were only about one hundred and fifty students when Mandela was there, and it was an incubator not only of traditional tribal leaders but future revolutionaries like Mandela. The students tended to be young men like Nelson, from well-to-do aristocratic African families, or black students who had excelled at missionary schools. They were well-mannered, wore suits, and the rules were strict. The school was run by Alexander Kerr, a stern and erudite Scotsman who was tough on the boys but proud of what the school represented. Mandela's nephew from the Thembu royal house, K. D. Matanzima, was an upperclassman: a tall proud fellow who was not only older than Mandela but was in line to be a chief. Mandela idolized him.

Mandela was a popular student at Fort Hare: bright, personable, athletic, fair. During his second year, Mandela took part in a protest about something more prosaic than prejudice: the food. The students protesting the poor quality of the food decided to boycott the student election. But a number of students did vote, and Mandela was elected to the student council. This troubled him. He had not been elected by a majority, and he believed that the result was not legitimate. Dr. Kerr insisted that Mandela and the others who had been elected serve on the council and gave Mandela an ultimatum: either serve on the council or leave Fort Hare. As he said to me in recalling the incident, "I was frightened and I went and reported to K. D. and he said it doesn't matter. It is a question of principle. Just tell them you are not going to serve. So I went in to Kerr—I feared K. D. more than I feared Dr. Kerr." Kerr told him that he needed to make a choice. Mandela stuck to his principles and left the school.

Mandela related the story with a smile and a chuckle. He was smiling at the headstrong young man who had made a choice that Mandela would never make today, nor advise anyone else to make. That young man had given up an educational advantage that would have made him a more powerful force in fighting discrimination. All principles are not created equal. You have to weigh the relative advantages. Here the principle was trifling and the sacrifice was significant. The cost far outweighed the benefit.

In some ways, that decision set him on a lifetime course of challenging authority. When he returned to Mqhekezweni, he dreaded telling the king what had happened. When he did, the king was both bewildered and enraged by Mandela's story. It was shortly thereafter that Mandela and his cousin Justice ran away to Johannesburg.

\# \# \#

Mandela's early years in Johannesburg read like a picaresque novel: working as a night watchman in a mine and getting fired; living in a succession of shanties without electricity; being regarded by his host families as a backward wastrel. It was only when he met the man who would become his lifelong friend and mentor, Walter Sisulu, that he began to straighten himself out. Through Walter he got a job as a clerk in a small Jewish law firm in Johannesburg—one of the few that would hire an African paralegal. For Mandela, the law seemed to be a way out, a meritocratic means of rising in the world, and he enrolled in a course of legal study at the University of Witwatersrand. He recalls with a smile his law professor there, who said that people of color were not bright enough to become attorneys.

The practice that Mandela eventually started with his friend and colleague Oliver Tambo became the first black law firm in South Africa and the place for the black elite to seek legal counsel. Mandela was an aggressive and dynamic presence in the courtroom and he fought against many apartheid laws for his clients. He was proud of his skill as a lawyer and trusted in the clear symmetries of legal statutes.

Although his legal education taught him that justice was blind—indeed, there was a statue of blind justice standing outside the court where he tried most of his cases—he began to see too much evidence to the contrary. He tried cases where judges evaluated the racial classification of his clients by the slope of their shoulders or by whether a pencil would stay in their hair. He tried cases where white defendants got off because of the color of their skin and black defendants were convicted because of theirs. And he saw, day in and day out, how the government used the law to repress the ANC and the freedom movement. "In actual practice," he wrote in his unpublished diary, "law is nothing but organized force used by the ruling class to shape the social order in a way favourable to itself." He reluctantly concluded that the law was not about immutable moral principles of equal justice, as he had once believed; it was a tactic to be used for his own political ends.

Mandela's early years as a member of the ANC Youth League were a constant conflict between principles and tactics. He first opposed allowing nonblacks to be members of the ANC on principle, then changed his mind. He then opposed allowing members of the Communist Party to belong to the ANC, and then changed his mind. In each case, pragmatism won out over principle. In each case, his decision was about which course would ultimately help the ANC become stronger.

The most significant example of strategy trumping principle was Mandela's and the ANC's embrace of violence as a part of the freedom struggle. From the time the ANC was formed in 1912, nonviolent protest had been at the core of its mission. For decades, the leaders of the ANC had been deeply influenced by the example of Gandhi, and nonviolence was an unshakable tenet of their organization.

But after seeing the government's consistent use of violence in repressing black protest, Mandela grew impatient with nonviolence. He felt as though he was carrying a spear to a gunfight. Finally, in 1961, Mandela journeyed to Natal to discuss a change of course with Chief Albert Luthuli, who was then the president of the ANC and who had won the Nobel Peace Prize the year before for leading the nonviolent struggle against apartheid. Mandela had immense respect for "The Chief," as he called him, and I asked Mandela what Luthuli's response was to the change in strategy.

"He of course opposed that decision because he was a man who believed in nonviolence as a principle," Mandela recalled. "Whereas I and others believed in nonviolence as a strategy, which could be changed at any time the conditions demanded it. So that was the difference between us."

Many of the Indian members of the ANC were adamant about not abandoning nonviolence. Mandela recalled that J. N. Singh, the great Indian freedom fighter, fought the change. "J. N. kept on saying, with great eloquence, 'No, nonviolence has not failed us, *we* have failed nonviolence.' And these slogans, you know, can be very powerful." But for him, the opposition had become a slogan, not a principle. In his hardheaded way, he had concluded that only a violent guerilla movement had a chance of toppling apartheid. "It is a question of the conditions which prevail, whether you have to use peaceful methods or violent methods. And that is determined purely by the conditions," he told me.

Conditions plus principles determine strategy. Mandela is not and never was a Gandhi, a man whose devotion to nonviolence was a life principle that if violated would make the victory not worth having. Yes, Mandela preferred nonviolence—and had a personal revulsion toward violence of any kind—but the policy of nonviolence was undermining the one overarching principle that he could never lose sight of.

Mandela was always proud of the correspondence college degrees that political prisoners earned on Robben Island. In later years, many political prisoners referred to the Island as The University. Robben Island was Mandela's university as well, but it was not an academic education. There he learned to be realistic, not abstract; to examine all principles in the light of conditions on the ground. In prison, he and his comrades spent hours, days, months, and years discussing theoretical issues: capitalism versus socialism, tribalism versus modernism, even whether the tiger was indigenous to the

African continent; and Mandela participated actively in these debates.

But when he emerged from prison, he put all abstract debates aside. He realized quickly that socialism would undermine his quest for democracy and racial harmony, and that tribalism could be useful to him. He made peace with the white capitalist chiefs and he made peace with the black tribal chiefs. Once he had achieved his great goal of bringing constitutional democracy to South Africa, he embraced its corollary: achieving racial harmony. Everything else was subordinate to those overriding goals. When conditions change, you must change your strategy and your mind. That's not indecisiveness, that's pragmatism.

7

See the Good
in Others

S OME CALL IT A BLIND SPOT, others naïveté, but Mandela sees almost everyone as virtuous until proven otherwise. He starts with an assumption that you are dealing with him in good faith. He believes that, just as pretending to be brave can lead to acts of real bravery, seeing the good in other people improves the chances that they will reveal their better selves.

It is extraordinary that a man who was ill-treated for most of his life can see so much good in others. In fact, it was sometimes frustrating to talk with him because he almost never had a bad word to say about anyone. He would not even say a disapproving word about the man who tried to have him hanged. I once asked him about John Vorster, the Nazi-sympathizing president of South Africa who tightened apartheid and rued the fact that Mandela and his comrades had not been executed.

"He was a very decent chap," Mandela said with complete sincerity. "In the first place, he was very polite. In referring to us, he used courteous terminology."

This might seem like praising Saddam Hussein because he was kind to animals. But it is not that Mandela does not see the dark side of someone like John Vorster; it is that he is unwilling to see *only* that. He knows that no one is purely good or purely evil. We were talking one day about a prisoner who had been a rival of Mandela's on Robben Island and who had actually put together a list of grievances about Mandela. When I asked him about the fellow, Mandela did not address the man's hostility but said, "What I took from him was his ability to work hard . . ."

What I took from him. Mandela seeks out the positive, the constructive. He chooses to look past the negative. He does this for two reasons: because he instinctively sees the good in people and because he intellectually believes that seeing the good in others might actually make them better. If you expect more of people, whether they are coworkers or family members, they often contribute more. Or at least feel guilty if they do not.

The worst he might say about someone is that they are operating in their own self-interest. I remember once listening to him talk on the phone with the editor of South Africa's largest black newspaper. The editor was planning to run a piece on the negotiations, and Mandela asked him to hold off because the matter was sensitive. Afterward, Mandela assured me that the editor would pull the story. The following day, though, the story was as big as life on the front page. I pointed it out to him, and he smiled and said, "These people do these things, you see, without an ulterior motive. They do it from the point of view of their own interest. So I didn't get cross about it." The editor had not misled him; he had simply acted in his own interest. There was no point in taking it personally. And he didn't.

\#   \#   \#

In a curious way, prison opened up Mandela's view of human nature rather than constricting it. While prison embittered many other men, it broadened Mandela. During those early years on Robben Island, when prisoners were routinely beaten and assaulted, when there was almost no communication with the outside world and such violations went unreported, the head of the island was Colonel Piet Badenhorst, a man with a reputation for icy brutality. Badenhorst was considered the worst example of the unreconstructed Afrikaner prison head, a man who believed that the black prisoners were little more than animals and should be treated as such. He regarded the political prisoners as terrorists and Mandela as terrorist number one. Mandela butted heads with him on many occasions and found him unmovable.

In the early 1970s, a group of judges visited the Island, and Mandela was asked by his fellow prisoners to present their grievances. "There had just been an attack, a beating-up of our people in another section," Mandela told me. Upon their arrival the judges—who tended to be English-speaking and more liberal than the prison officials—told Mandela that the meeting would not include Badenhorst so that Mandela could speak freely. Mandela said that he thought it was proper for Badenhorst to be there and that it would not intimidate him. At the meeting, Mandela began to relate a story of a recent assault. Badenhorst jumped in and asked, "Did you actually witness the assault?" Mandela replied that he had not. At that point, Badenhorst pointed his finger at Mandela and said, "Be careful. Don't talk about things you haven't seen or you will get in serious trouble." There was a silence, at which point Mandela turned to the judges and calmly said, "You can see what type of commanding officer we have. If he threatens me in your presence, you can imagine what he does when you are not here."

Mandela told that story to illustrate the worst side of Badenhorst. But then he quickly segued to a second story about when Badenhorst left the Island. Mandela was summoned to see General J. C. Steyn, the head of the prison system, who was making one of his occasional visits. Steyn was joined by Badenhorst, and the general asked Mandela whether he had any complaints. Mandela, in his deliberate, lawyerly way, began to list the prisoners' grievances. He was never diffident about stating his case and that of his comrades in front of the authorities. When he was done, Steyn said that he had some news for Mandela: Colonel Badenhorst was being transferred from Robben Island. Mandela recalled that Badenhorst then turned and spoke to him directly.

"Badenhorst said to me something like, 'I just want to wish you people good luck.' He said this like a human being, and I was a bit taken aback by his moderate and even considerate tone. I must say, that was a bit of a surprise. I thanked him. I thought about this for a long time afterward. What it basically showed me is that these men were not inhuman, but their inhumanity had been put upon them. They behaved like beasts because they were rewarded for such behavior. They thought it would result in a promotion or advancement. That day, I realized that Badenhorst was not the man he seemed to be, but a better man than how he had behaved."

This epiphany goes to the heart of Mandela's belief

about what makes us human. He was *a better man than how he had behaved*. His motives were not as cruel as his actions. No one is born prejudiced or racist. No man, he suggests, is evil at heart. Evil is something instilled in or taught to men by circumstances, their environment, or their upbringing. It is not innate. Apartheid made men evil; evil did not create apartheid.

While his colleagues saw their warders and jailers as monolithic, the embodiment of the heartless apartheid system, Mandela generally tried to find something decent and honorable in them. Ultimately, he came to see them as victims of the system as well as perpetrators of it. As he often told me, they were simple, uneducated men who had been inculcated in an unfair and racist system since they were children. Almost all were from poor families—an upbringing not all that different from most of the prisoners. As an educated, widely read attorney who had made one trip around Africa, Mandela had already seen far more of the world than these guards would ever see. They had suffered under the apartheid system too, albeit not in the same way as Mandela and his colleagues.

Mandela took a similar view of the Reverend André Scheffer, who preached to the prisoners on Sundays. Scheffer was a fire-and-brimstone preacher from the

Dutch Reformed Church who believed, who *knew,* that the separation of races had been ordained by God. "He was very contemptuous, very abusive," Mandela recalled. Scheffer saw Mandela and his colleagues as common criminals, men who were trying to subvert a fair and theologically justified system.

"'You think you are freedom fighters,'" Mandela recalled him saying. "'You must have been drunk with *dagga* [marijuana] and liquor when you were arrested. You people have got an easy answer whenever there is a problem, you say, *Ngabelungu* [It's the whites].'"

The other prisoners found the Reverend insufferable and would do anything to avoid his presence. But Mandela saw him as a challenge. In his view, religious beliefs were imposed on people in the same way that apartheid was; the minister's zeal was simply a reflection of how he had been raised. Mandela saw past the jeremiads and glimpsed a human being behind the bluster. So, while the minister was trying to convert them, he began trying to convert the minister.

"We worked on him," Mandela told me. "I wanted him to preach to us. We were always trying to convert people to our cause. Over time, we explained to him who we were, why we were in prison, what we stood for." According to Mandela, Scheffer became friendlier and came at least to understand why they were fighting. He never became a believer, but he was no longer their enemy. Mandela had won him over.

Mandela's comrades generally indulged his some-times benign view of the guards, but among themselves they criticized him for being too trusting, too willing to see the good in those whom they regarded as irre-deemable. Why try to understand your enemy, they would say, one must simply defeat him. Some said that Mandela was naïve, that his open-mindedness was a form of intellectual weakness. He was too susceptible to kindness, they complained, too willing to do the bidding of any guard who addressed him politely. They saw it as a hunger for status. And there were those among his comrades who went even further: They said these were not mere personality flaws, but that Mandela was guilty of appeasing the enemy.

Mandela was aware of this criticism, but he con-sciously chose to err on the side of generosity. He even felt the same way about those who criticized him. By be-having honorably, even to people who may not deserve it, he believes you can influence them to behave more honorably than they otherwise would. This sometimes proved to be a useful tactic, particularly after he was re-leased from prison, when his open, trusting attitude made him appear to be a man who could rise above bitterness. When he urged South Africans to "forget the past," most of them believed that he had. This had a double effect: It made whites trust Mandela more and it made them feel more generous toward the people they had so recently oppressed.

* * *

To Mandela, it pays to trust people, but even he admits to having trusted people who he feels betrayed him. The person he most regretted trusting to the extent that he did was F. W. de Klerk, the man who released him from prison, the man with whom he eventually shared a Nobel Peace Prize. From the first, as Mandela recalled, de Klerk treated him with "great courtesy," always a way to ingratiate oneself with Mandela. Early on, Mandela called him "a man of integrity," a phrase he would come to regret at the height of their negotiations.

Mandela met with de Klerk on three occasions before de Klerk agreed to release him and lift the ban on the ANC. From the first, Mandela perceived him as a different kind of National Party leader. He described him as "courageous" for having started the reform process. Mandela was still at Victor Verster prison when he first met with de Klerk at the presidential retreat in Cape Town. He congratulated de Klerk on becoming state president, and then took him to task for proposing a policy on "group rights" that he described as bringing "apartheid through the back door." According to Mandela, de Klerk said that if Mandela did not want the policy, he would not pursue it. "I was tremendously impressed," Mandela told me. In many ways, de Klerk used the same strategy with Mandela that Mandela had used with the prison guards and with de Klerk's predecessors. He treated Mandela with great courtesy, was amenable, and behaved as though they were men cut from the same cloth.

I was with them on a number of occasions, and de Klerk was warm yet formal with Mandela. He would call him Mr. Mandela in his sonorous baritone. De Klerk, who was a chain-smoker, even tried not to smoke in Mandela's presence, as Mandela did not care for cigarette smoke. Mandela did not recognize de Klerk's behavior as part of a strategy meant to disarm him. He himself suffered from the same blind spot he recognized and exploited in others.

But after Mandela's release, as the negotiations over elections and a new constitution began in earnest, Mandela's view of de Klerk began to change. Mandela believed that the government was supporting what he called "the Third Force," a shadowy paramilitary organization that was fomenting violence and attempting to trigger a civil war. Mandela believed de Klerk knew about this and condoned it, though there is no evidence of his involvement and de Klerk has always disputed it. The men quarreled in public and in private, and Mandela came to see de Klerk as two-faced and hypocritical.

De Klerk sparked one of Mandela's only moments of public anger. It was December 1991, and both men were set to speak at a public ceremony signaling the opening of their historic talks regarding South Africa's first democratic constitution. These negotiations would be critical in eventually leading to South Africa's first "one person, one vote" election in 1994. Mandela told me that de Klerk had come to him privately and asked to speak last. Mandela had agreed. Mandela spoke first and adopted a tone of goodwill, speaking of his hopes for the constitutional talks. But when de Klerk spoke, there was no olive branch. Instead he took the ANC and Mandela to task for maintaining what he described as secret armies that were causing violence in the country. He essentially accused Mandela—who had so often spoken to de Klerk in private of his own concerns about the Third Force—of being a hypocrite. Mandela regarded every word of what de Klerk spoke as a lie. When de Klerk finished speaking, the conference was meant to be over, but

Mandela got up from his desk and in front of live television cameras strode to the podium. His face was a rictus of cold fury. He did not look at de Klerk as he spoke.

"Even the head of an illegitimate, discredited minority regime, as his is, has certain moral standards to uphold . . . . If a man can come to a conference of this nature and play this type of politics—very few people would like to deal with such a man."

It was the angriest I have ever seen him, and it was clear that he was using every ounce of his immense self-discipline to keep himself under control. The two men had made a gentleman's agreement, and he felt he had been gracious in agreeing to let de Klerk end the conference. Now he felt betrayed—all the more so because he places such a high value on courtesy and reciprocal good behavior.

Several years later, I had a conversation with Mandela about de Klerk and I could see that the wounds had begun to heal. He said that de Klerk had simply acted in his own interest and that of his political followers—but that he had been disappointed that de Klerk had not risen above it. He had misjudged him, he admitted, but he had not been wrong to trust him. De Klerk had been a necessary partner on the road to freedom, and Mandela saw no utility in denying that he had been a man of integrity. After all, there was no telling whether he would need de Klerk for something, so why alienate him?

Mandela sees the good in others both because it is in his nature and in his interest. At times that has meant being blindsided, but he has always been willing to take that risk. And it *is* a risk. We tend to think of risk as physical daring, like attempting a dangerous climb, or as making a decision with an uncertain outcome, like putting our money into an investment that is not a sure thing. But Mandela believes in and takes *emotional* risks. He goes out on a limb and makes himself vulnerable by trusting others. We sometimes do that by confiding in others we don't know well. Yet we rarely equate risk with trying to see what is decent, honest, and good in the people in our daily lives.

"People will feel I see too much good in people," Mandela once told me. "So it's a criticism I have to put up with, and I've tried to adjust because whether it is so or not, it is something I think is profitable. It's a good thing to assume, to act on the basis that others are men of integrity and honor, because you tend to attract integrity and honor if that is how you regard those with whom you work. I believe in that."

8

Know Your Enemy

IN THE 1950s, Mandela was a crusading attorney by day and an amateur boxer by night. He trained almost every evening at a spartan gym in the black township of Orlando. He was six-foot-two, stocky, a bit ponderous—never destined to be a champion heavyweight. But he was enormously disciplined and relished the training—skipping rope, distance running, the heavy bag—more than the fighting. His fiery coach, Skipper Molotsi, taught him that for a boxer to succeed, he not only had to be nimble and strong, he had to get to know his opponent. That meant learning how his rival followed a jab with a left hook, or whether he moved to the right or to the left after taking a punch.

Mandela realized he needed to do that in the political arena too. In order to defeat a resolute political opponent, he would have to understand him and discover his weaknesses. Mandela was the underdog and would also need to use his opponent's strength against him.

In 1962, when he was forty-four years old, Mandela

took the lead in founding Spear of the Nation (known as MK), the military wing of the ANC. He was MK's first commander in chief. As MK began to initiate some bombings of military targets, Mandela went underground and became an outlaw, South Africa's most wanted man, a shadowy figure whom white newspapers dubbed the Black Pimpernel. He grew a scraggly beard and wore old overalls, drove a car while wearing a baggy cap so that people thought he was a chauffeur or a garden boy. He began to learn about warfare, reading Sun Tzu's *The Art of War* and any kind of military manual he could get his hands on.

He also began studying manuals of a different kind: handbooks of Afrikaans grammar.

His comrades could understand his studying *The Art of War* but not the art of Afrikaans poetry. They used to tease him about learning the language of the oppressor. But Mandela knew he could not defeat his enemy if he did not understand him, and that he could not understand him if he did not speak his language. Literally. And he was thinking even further ahead: There could be no dispensation in South Africa, no peaceful resolution of the conflict that did not somehow include the Afrikaner. Even as head of MK, he did not envision driving Afrikaners into the sea; there would eventually need to be accommodation and negotiation.

When I asked him why he had started studying Afrikaans, he gave a very forthright answer. "Well, it's obvious because as a public figure, you do want to know the two main languages of the country, and Afrikaans is an important language spoken by the majority of the white population in the country and by the majority of the Colored people, and it's a disadvantage not to know it." He paused, then added: "When you speak Afrikaans, you know, you go straight to their hearts."

You go straight to their hearts. It was an echo of something else he had famously said about the art of persuasion: "Don't address their brains. Address their hearts." This is true in many arenas of our lives—whether we are trying to persuade a colleague to see our point of view, win someone's vote, or attract new customers. If you want to make the sale, address the heart. Mandela did this with his own supporters as well as the Afrikaner. But in the case of the Afrikaner, he had much more to overcome. Mandela knew that prejudice was not rational and that he could not address it only in a rational way. He needed whites to accept democracy and the idea of a diverse nation not only intellectually but emotionally. Only then would he achieve the accommodation he truly sought. He had always appealed to people's minds, but he knew that his ultimate victory would only come when he won over their hearts.

❋　❋　❋

In 1962, about a year and a half after going under-ground—and only a few months after he started studying Afrikaans—Mandela was arrested crossing the border from Botswana into South Africa. Once captured, he would eventually be put on trial for treason with the possibility of the death sentence. Many thought that the infamous Rivonia Trial, which stretched out for nearly a year, would be the last they would ever see or hear of Nelson Mandela. During the early days of the trial, Mandela recalls talking to "a friendly Afrikaans warder" about the case.

"[He] asked me the question, 'Mandela, what do you think the judge is going to do with you in this case?' and I said, 'Agh, hang us.' I really did not mean that. I wanted some support and sympathy from him. I thought he was going to say, 'Agh, I think he'll never do that.' But he stopped, became serious and took his eyes away from me, looked down, and he says, 'I think you're right, they're going to hang you.'"

It was an insight into the heart of his enemy. The Afrikaner was very direct, very straightforward, not wily or sly. He could be sympathetic or not, but he was going to tell you what was on his mind.

In the end, the judge sentenced him and his colleagues to life in prison. The night of the sentencing, he and his fellow black defendants were packed into a van, put on a plane to Cape Town, and taken to Robben Island. It was there, in his first few years on the Island, that Mandela began to seriously study the language of his judge and jailers. He enrolled in a correspondence course in Afrikaans, and Afrikaans grammar manuals were among the few books he was allowed during those harsh early years. (His request for a copy of Tolstoy's *War and Peace* was rejected because the authorities thought it was a military manual.) And he took almost every opportunity he could to speak to the guards in Afrikaans.

Many of his comrades could not understand it; to them, Mandela was showing deference to the oppressor by speaking his language. And while his fellow prisoners did not appreciate his efforts, the guards did. Their English was clumsy, and many of the other prisoners either did not speak Afrikaans or refused to. Mandela's willingness to converse with them in Afrikaans soon bore fruit. Before long, warders were coming up to his window during the night and seeking his advice.

"Without boasting," he said to me, "they normally came, especially during the weekend and in the evenings, to talk to me. Some of them were really good men and expressed their views uncompromisingly about the treatment we were receiving."

In part by touching their hearts, he converted some of his enemies into his allies. To him, the warders were a microcosm of the Afrikaans population as a whole, and if he could win over these poorly educated and often prejudiced men, he could win over a whole people.

Mandela realized that he not only had to learn the language, he had to comprehend the culture. So he memorized Afrikaans poetry and read deeply in Afrikaner history. He knew that Afrikaners were not only proud of their frontier history, but of their military prowess. They cherished the names of the Boer generals who had fought off troops of the British Empire during the Anglo-Boer War, at a time when Britain was the greatest military power on the planet. He learned the names of famous Boer generals and the stories of their derring-do. His reading of Afrikaner military history also taught him something of the way they fought: how resourceful and wily they were, how determined and bloody-minded. Decades later, when he began negotiations with the leaders of the government, those men would be amazed and impressed by Mandela's references to Afrikaner generals and battles.

On Robben Island, Mandela would tell his comrades that Afrikaners were Africans too. They were people of Dutch, German, and other European ancestry who had immigrated to Africa, cutting their ties with

Europe. The Afrikaner no longer had a homeland elsewhere. He was a transplant now firmly rooted in Africa, just like the hardy and beautiful Jacaranda tree, which had come from Europe and had long since become a symbol of South African culture.

Mandela understood that there were profound similarities between the African and the Afrikaner. Both suffered from a sense of insecurity. Both had been oppressed by the British. Afrikaners had been demeaned by the British imperialists, treated as boorish second-class citizens only a step up from Africans. They too felt like scorned outsiders. As a people, they had a collective chip on their shoulder, not so different from the black South Africans under apartheid.

While Mandela never became chummy with the warders on Robben Island, over the years they began to treat him and his fellow prisoners with more respect and some deference. Years later, when he was transferred to Pollsmoor prison, Mandela would have more freedom, including a private cell, but he endured a more difficult commander. Major Fritz Van Sittert was used to dealing with common criminals, not political prisoners, much less the most famous political prisoner in the world. He cut them no slack, and he was unhappy that Mandela received any special treatment whatsoever.

Still, Mandela believed that he could win over

anyone, and he made a study of Van Sittert. He discovered that Van Sittert was obsessed with rugby. Rugby was the Afrikaner's national sport, something close to a civil religion. It was a source of pride that gave them a sense of distinctiveness. They adored the Springboks, the national team, which was made up mainly of large and powerful Afrikaners wearing the team's distinctive green and yellow uniforms. The sport seemed to mirror the tribe: brutal, fast, intense, and played with no pads or helmets.

For all these reasons, black freedom fighters had always despised the sport, regarding it as a symbol of Afrikaner brutality. Black South Africans routinely rooted for whatever country was playing against the Springboks (as the saying goes, the enemy of my enemy is my friend), regarding a defeat of the national team as a victory against apartheid.

But Mandela now saw rugby as a way of getting through to Major Van Sittert. Van Sittert came to see him once a month, and to prepare for his visits, Mandela began to read the sports pages, concentrating on the rugby scores, learning the names of the players and their talents. Initially, Van Sittert was quite curt with Mandela, and was intent on doing him no favors. Mandela's guard at Pollsmoor, Christo Brand, recalled how Mandela began to converse with Van Sittert in Afrikaans and talk about rugby. Soon, Brand recalls, this penetrated Van Sittert's hostile reserve, and he began swapping rugby stories and observations with his prisoner.

By the time Mandela got to Victor Verster Prison in 1988, not only was his Afrikaans better, but he had his own private residence and a cook, Warrant Officer Jack Swart. Swart was a tall, loose-limbed fellow with a thick salt-and-pepper moustache. He cooked three meals a day for Mandela, who became very fond of him. "He would cook the most lovely meals," Mandela said, describing him as a "progressive chap—no color bar at all." Mandela recalls how they used to argue over doing the dishes; Mandela would insist, and Swart would say that it was his job. Mandela did them anyway.

I went to see Swart, who become the cook for the whole prison after Mandela was released. He was a rather gruff fellow, but it was obvious that he had great affection for Mandela. The two men were alike in many ways: deliberate, careful, abstemious. When I asked what language they spoke to each other, Swart finally smiled. "I would talk in English," he said, "and he would talk in Afrikaans." I asked him why. "We did it so I could improve my English and he could improve his Afrikaans." How was Mandela's Afrikaans? Again, he smiled. "Good. He spoke it slowly." Mandela's Afrikaans was precise and bookish; he regarded that precision as a form of respect.

* * *

In Chapter 3, I wrote about how Mandela was taken from prison to meet with P. W. Botha, the president of South Africa. Even before he knew the meeting was set, Mandela began to prepare. He learned as much about Botha as he could. He carefully planned what to say and for weeks he practiced his lines. Like a great actor, he rehearsed and made the role his own.

Despite his preparation, Mandela was extremely tense. He had been warned that Botha was hot-tempered, and he was prepared for a fight. The stakes could not have been higher. The ANC has been in existence for seven decades, but this would be the first time one of its leaders met with the president of South Africa. This one meeting could set the stage for a peaceful path to a nonracial democracy or a bloody civil war. If it did not go well, it could also lead to Mandela being treated as a pariah by his political comrades.

On the day of the meeting, Mandela awoke very early and was ready hours before he needed to leave. He was driven to the stately residence of the president,

Tuynhuys in Cape Town, and he was ushered into the dining room by the head of the intelligence service and Justice Minister Kobie Coetsee. Coetsee straightened Mandela's tie (Mandela had lost the knack in prison) and kneeled down to tighten Mandela's shoelaces.

"As I entered, feeling very tense, the president entered from his door. We came at just the same time; he was apparently timing me," Mandela said. Botha, he said, "was full of smiles and with his hand out." Mandela strode confidently forward with his hand outstretched, greeting Botha in Afrikaans. Botha responded and asked him if he would have some tea, which Botha poured for him. While sipping tea together, Mandela revealed to Botha that he was knowledgeable about Afrikaner history in general, and about the Anglo-Boer War in particular. He reeled off the names of famous Boer generals. He recalled some famous battles. Botha was clearly enjoying himself.

After he had loosened Botha up, Mandela used his knowledge of Afrikaner history to make a serious and less pleasant point. During World War II, South Africa was led by the English-speaking United Party, not the Afrikaans-speaking National Party. When the country declared war on Germany, Afrikaners fiercely objected. The Afrikaner leaders were profoundly anti-British and were so determined not to ally themselves with the

British that they preferred to side with Britain's enemy, Germany. Mandela pointedly told Botha, "They had occupied many towns in the Free State and destroyed property, killing three hundred people. Nevertheless, the leader of the rebellion was released before he had completed six months."

Mandela's purpose here was not only to show Botha that he was a student of Afrikaner history but to make clear that there were parallels between the Afrikaner rebellion against Britain and the ANC's struggle against apartheid. But he had also slyly noted that the government freed the rebels within six months of their capture, and that he and his colleagues had been in prison for more than two decades. When Mandela then asked Botha to release Walter Sisulu—something Botha had publicly refused to do—the president promptly agreed.

Afrikaners are blunt and they respect bluntness in others. Mandela was both blunt and courteous, a combination Botha could understand, for that is exactly the way he was.

\# \# \#

Rugby came back into Mandela's life when he became president. Job number one for him was to be the father of the nation, the patriarch who united white and black around a common vision. There were times, claimed some of his critics, that he seemed to spend more time easing white fears than relieving black hardship. But he knew there was a powerful counterrevolutionary movement among right-wing Afrikaners, and he believed that rather than clamping down on them, he could win them over. And if he could not win over the far right, he could at least win over the Afrikaners in the middle who might otherwise have been tempted to support them.

When the threats to harmony were greatest, in 1994 and 1995, Mandela used a curious tactic: He turned to sports as a way of healing the nation. For years, the ANC had done everything it could to get the Springboks, the national rugby team, banned from international play. And they had succeeded. Now Mandela sought to have the ban on them lifted, and he became instrumental in bringing the rugby World Cup to South Africa. He thought rugby could be the great uniter, and not a divider. He began a charm campaign to win over the rugby establishment. He befriended Francois Pienaar, the six-foot-seven Springbok captain, who fell under his spell. He made a number of visits to the team, rugged Afrikaners who at best were apolitical and who were mistrustful of a black leader and black politics. The day before the Springboks were to play the reigning champion, Australia, in May 1995, Mandela flew to their training camp to tell them they were playing for the whole country and that the whole nation, white and black, was behind them. He put on the Springbok cap. As the team manager later told journalist John Carlin, "He had won their hearts."

In his most famous gesture of reconciliation, Mandela wore the Springbok jersey and cap to the rugby finals at Johannesburg's Ellis Park Stadium in 1995. When he strode out before the game to greet the team captain, the mostly white crowd began to chant, "Nelson, Nel-son!" It was one of the most electrifying moments in the history of sport and politics. Tokyo Sexwale, who had been imprisoned with Mandela on Robben Island, told Carlin, "That was the moment when I understood more clearly than ever before that the liberation struggle was not so much about liberating blacks from bondage, it was about liberating white people from fear."

Ultimately, for Mandela, knowing the enemy was not only a tactical act, but an act of empathy. Mandela would never say, as the comic strip character Pogo famously did, "We have met the enemy and he is us." But he was so intent on winning them over that that in itself engendered a kind of loyalty to him. Afrikaners saw the effort Mandela had made; he had come more than halfway to meet them when he had not needed to move at all. In the end, Afrikaners understood that and came to trust him. He won their hearts.

And when you have won over your enemy, Mandela said, never gloat. The time of your greatest triumph is the time when you should be most merciful. Do not humiliate them under any circumstances. Let them, in fact, save face. And then, Mandela said, you will have made your enemy your friend.

9

Keep Your Rivals Close

WHILE MANDELA OFTEN TOOK his friends for granted, he never did the same with his rivals. While he often lost track of his colleagues, he never stopped tracking his opponents. You can trust your friends, in the sense that you roughly know that they will support you, and you can trust your enemies, in the sense that you assume that they will always oppose you. But your friendly rivals—they are the ones you need to keep tabs on. And Mandela always did.

He did it discreetly. He would not have considered using intelligence services or private eyes to spy on his rivals. He knew that the best way to do that was not from a distance but from up close. In fact, when they were in a room together, he would often motion for a rival to come over and sit next to him, all the better to keep an eye on him.

Plotting out the moves of his rivals is one example of how meticulously Mandela prepares. We are sometimes urged to expect the unexpected, to prepare ourselves for the least likely outcome in any situation. Mandela would say we need to do a better job of expecting the *expected*, that we often do not prepare for those things we know are likely to be coming. For him, one of those things was a rival who would challenge you.

Mandela was almost always the center of attention in any room that he was in, and he liked that. His posture was that of a man whose image is on a coin—proud, confident, chin raised high. And when he was holding court he would look from eye to eye and try to win you over. But in those moments when the spotlight was not on him, you could catch him watching and evaluating others. His eyes were not on his friends, but on those he considered rivals or potential rivals. He observed their style, their mode of speaking, even their way of shaking hands. He once told me that a certain member of his cabinet would not look him in the eye when shaking hands, and that was not a good sign.

Mandela, unlike many politicians and leaders, never made a god out of loyalty. He expected it and was disappointed when it was not given, but he knew that loyalty in politics and life was usually circumstantial. There was no such thing as absolute loyalty. Loyalty was in large part self-interest, and he wanted to make his rivals think it was in their interest to be loyal—or at the least, give them less room to be disloyal.

Despite his vigilance, Mandela was not always a good judge of character. His commitment to seeing the good in others meant that he was sometimes unable to see their dark side. He was also susceptible to flattery and glamour and wealth. But he had an eye for human frailty, and he was always on the lookout for those who made decisions that were impulsive and emotional rather than well thought out, probably because he had been that way himself as a young man. The young Nelson Mandela had been a threat to the older leadership of the ANC. So he was on the watch for such individuals, knowing that they had the potential to undermine his power and upset his plans.

In fact, tensions between the old and new guard of the African National Congress were apparent as soon as Mandela emerged from prison. He saw that there were two camps: the hardliners and the conciliators. The divide was generational, with the younger leaders being more aggressive and confrontational than those of Mandela's era. One of those young leaders was Bantu Holomisa, the general who in 1987 had led a military coup and taken over the leadership of the Transkei. Holomisa was in his late thirties, but looked even younger, and was a fireplug of a man with a winning smile and a sharp laugh. To my mind, he was a curious combination of a traditional leader and revolutionary—ambitious and hotheaded, susceptible to the arguments of those on the left who saw Mandela as too willing to compromise, too trusting of the government. Mandela saw Holomisa as being vulnerable to malign influences.

When we were in the Transkei, Mandela always wanted Holomisa around. "Where is Bantu?" he would say. "Where is the general?" When Holomisa entered Mandela's living room, Mandela would pat the chair next to him and say, "Ah, General, come sit next to me." He would hold hands with Holomisa, a tradition among African men but not one Mandela often practiced. He publicly treated Holomisa as a son—and far better than his own sons, with whom he was quite reserved.

In private, Mandela told me that Holomisa was a loose cannon who needed to be monitored. And that was precisely what Mandela did. He did not make a move in the Transkei without inviting Holomisa along. Holomisa loved that. The idea was to co-opt him by making him feel important and indispensable, and indeed Holomisa seemed to expand with pleasure and pride when Mandela held his hand or put his arm around him. He would often ask me, "Does the old man seem happy?" and he would beam when I said yes. Just as we ingratiate ourselves with people by asking for favors rather than doing them, Mandela ingratiated himself with Holomisa by seeming to be dependent on him. Holomisa, as a result, felt more loyal to the old man.

Mandela treated Chris Hani almost exactly the same way, and for the same reasons. Before his assassination, Hani was one of the most popular young leaders in South Africa precisely because he was so militant and fierce. There were untold millions of blacks in South Africa for whom vengeance was more appealing than reconciliation, who could not and did not want to forget the past as Mandela urged them to do. Mandela was asking them to turn the other cheek, to be patient and forgiving. That is not easy for anyone, much less millions of disenfranchised people who had had a boot on their necks for generations.

Mandela saw in Hani the same anger and impatience that he himself felt when he was a young leader, and he was wary. Rather than pushing Hani away, he kept him close. When we were in Johannesburg, Mandela would always ask his aides to include Hani in meetings or trips, particularly ceremonial occasions. He would keep Hani next to him, hold his hand as he did with Holomisa. In part this was to watch over him, but in part it was shrewd political stagecraft, not unlike when an aging Hollywood leading man casts a young actor by his side to make himself seem more relevant and contemporary.

I remember once sitting with Hani while Mandela gave a speech outside Johannesburg. Mandela told the story of how he had gone to some of South Africa's "top industrialists"—he seemed very proud that he had access to them—and had asked them for money for the ANC. He told his listeners that he "did not want to leave this office without a check," and then added, "I was not disappointed." This was an anecdote he told quite often at the time, and while he thought it illustrated how white businessmen were trying to help the struggle, the reaction of the audience was that he was strong-arming the businessmen in a way that felt close to political blackmail.

I leaned over to Hani and said that I didn't think the anecdote was going over very well. He agreed; he had obviously been thinking the same thing. "Perhaps you should mention it to him," I said. He smiled, looked at me directly, and said, "Why don't you?" Hani was reluctant to say anything discouraging to Mandela; he was like the overawed son who did not want to confront the father. But in the end, that is what worried Mandela; he was more comfortable with those who confronted him than those who hid their feelings.

What Hani and Holomisa had in common is not so much that they were actively disloyal, but that they were "immature," that they made decisions based on "the blood" rather than the head. He saw this immaturity as a symptom of insecurity. These men, to his mind, suffered from a lack of confidence. Such men were unpredictable, dangerous, hard to rely on. To Mandela, there was active disloyalty, and then there was unpredictability. The two are not the same but overlap, for the emotional man is more likely to become the disloyal man, to make an error in judgment. There was no way to repair that insecurity; one simply had to take precautions.

※　　※　　※

The only two people I ever heard Mandela belittle in a way that revealed his own anger and bitterness were F. W. de Klerk and the Zulu leader Mangosuthu Buthelezi. While de Klerk fell into the category of the enemy who could become an ally, Buthelezi was an ostensible ally who could become an enemy. He was a clear rival to Mandela for leadership of South Africa—a rival who Mandela felt would be willing to lead the country to civil war in order to achieve his own ends.

Mandela's determination to see the good in others

did not extend to Buthelezi. I never heard him praise the Zulu chief. He found him mercurial and unreliable. He complained that Buthelezi negotiated man-to-man understandings with him, shook hands, and then backtracked on his promises.

Once, during a multiparty conference in 1991, Mandela spied Buthelezi with the young Zulu king on the other side of the room. Mandela walked clear across the room to shake hands with the king, and the king—at Buthelezi's insistence, according to Mandela—would not shake his hand. "He must have been a bit remorseful, because he later sent over an emissary who said the king did not shake hands with commoners. But then later I saw the king shake hands with de Klerk. I guess it's only black commoners he does not shake hands with," Mandela told me with a smile.

Given his clear distaste for Buthelezi, it came as a surprise to some when Mandela invited him into his first cabinet as minister of home affairs. But as he explained to me, he had done it precisely because he regarded the Zulu leader as so dangerous that he needed to "keep an eye on him." And where better to do that than in one's own cabinet? Although Mandela was not always a great actor, on the day of the press conference announcing Buthelezi's appointment, he acted as though the Zulu leader was a true statesman.

Mandela knew there was no fail-safe method of pre-empting attacks by rivals. But he believed that by taking a rival under his wing, he would make him at least think twice about it. And then, at least, he would be close enough to see it coming.

10

Know When to Say No

NELSON MANDELA IS NOT A MAN OF MAYBES. He may be silent. He may be evasive. He will sometimes delay and postpone and try to avoid you. But in the end, he will not tell you what you want to hear just because you want to hear it.

Even though he has an almost preternatural instinct to please, even though he hates to disappoint people, Nelson Mandela is very adept at saying no. There are times that he will say, "Let me think about it," but when he knows the answer is no he says so. This is not as easy or simple as it seems. We forget that *No* is a complete sentence.

He doesn't like to say it; you can see him struggling to get it out in a courteous way. But he knows that the price of not saying no now makes it even harder to say it later. Better to disappoint someone early. And he won't sugarcoat it or put it off on someone else. When saying no, he wants to be clear and definitive. He doesn't offer false hope or leave the door open just a crack.

There is a famous picture of him with Walter Sisulu on Robben Island in which Mandela is looking down and away from Walter, but pointing with his finger. That is how he says no—he averts his gaze for a moment to explain, and then he looks you in the eye and says, "Sorry, but the answer is no."

He has said many big and resolute nos in his political life. As a young man, he said no to having Communists in the ANC youth league. He said no to hiding his revolutionary acts in the Rivonia Trial. He said a giant no to President de Klerk when he thought de Klerk was trying to preserve white dominance of the government. In all these cases, the no represented the overarching principle; apart from that, almost anything else could be a yes or could be negotiated. And he knew that it was always possible to reverse himself.

I was often on the receiving end of Mandela's no. There were many times when I asked whether I could go to a meeting or on a trip or accompany him to a dinner. I would ask him directly, and there were times when he simply said yes, come on along. If the answer was no, he was never vague in his response. He never said, "I'll get back to you" or "I need to ask so-and-so." He would say, very quickly and clearly, "Richard, that is not a good idea," or, "I'm sorry, but that won't be possible." Nor did he couch his nos with false sympathy or excuses. He would never say, "Well, if not for X, the answer would be yes" or "Normally, I would want you to do this, but . . ." Making an excuse only gives the other person grounds for argument, and he understood from long experience that people cope better with a firm no than an ambiguous one.

At the same time, he did not say no when he did not have to. He was strategic about his nos. Why waste a no when you did not need to say no? Why be blunt when you do not have to be? Once he had just come back from a trip to the mountains of Montreux. He told me he had had a productive trip. I asked him whether he liked the mountains. He paused for a moment.

"I don't hate them," he said.

The answer is very Mandela-like. There was nothing to be gained by saying that he did not like the mountains, so why say it? Some voters love the mountains, so why alienate them unnecessarily? That is why he never would choose a team to root for. You only alienate the fans rooting for the other side. If something wasn't a direct question and he did not need to answer it, he usually didn't.

In general, he was relieved to not have to say no. As we were nearing the end of the interview process for his memoir, he was under a lot of pressure from his colleagues and the leadership of the ANC to campaign and negotiate full-time, without any distractions. He would tell me that we needed to speed up, and toward the end we booked two sessions a day, one in the early morning and one in the afternoon.

One day, I told him that I needed to speak to him seriously. I could see that this put him on guard, and he looked grave. We were sitting across from each other in identical wing chairs in the sunny living room of his house in Houghton. As I began to talk, he assumed his negotiating face: neutral, solemn, almost impossible to read. I told him that we were like two mountaineers nearing the summit of a great peak. It might still look far away, but if we turned around and looked back, we would see the vast distance we had traveled and how close we really were to the goal. He nodded with no expression. Then I said, "Here's my proposal. We do ten more hours of interviews, the final five on your life since the release."

The moment I finished he breathed deeply, thought for a moment, and then simply said, "Yes, very good." He seemed relieved. I know I was.

A week later, when I tried to wrangle a couple of extra hours, he wagged his finger at me and said no.

Throughout his life, Mandela had to make decisions about when to act and when not to, when to move ahead and when to abandon a position. Having spent so many years in prison, where he had a limited ability to affect things, he knew that many situations resolve themselves. There are some decisions that may benefit from delay— if you decide that's the case, then fine, don't worry about it. But if you are delaying or avoiding saying no because it is unpleasant, better to do it right away and clearly. You will avoid a heap of trouble in the long run.

11

It's a Long Game

TWENTY-SEVEN YEARS IN PRISON teaches you many things, but one of them is to play a long game. As a young man, Mandela was impatient: He wanted change yesterday. Prison taught him to slow down, and it reinforced his sense that haste often leads to error and misjudgment. Above all, he learned how to postpone gratification—his whole life embodies that.

Many of us are used to the opposite. Because our culture rewards speed, we see impatience as a virtue. We confuse instant gratification with expressing ourselves. We try to seize opportunity the moment it presents itself, to respond to every tweet or text message without stopping to think. But he would say that we should not let an illusion of urgency force us to make decisions before we are ready. It is true that there are times when we might miss out on an opportunity, if we do not turn on a dime. But there are also many times when we might make a better deal or do a better job if we act less quickly and play the long game. Better to be slow and considered than to be fast simply in order to appear decisive.

In Mandela's case, he knew that history isn't made overnight and that no one bends it with his own hands. Racism and repression had been incubated over millennia, colonialism had developed over centuries, apartheid had been created over decades, and none of it would be eradicated in a few months or even years. The man who went into prison was restless for an imagined future. To him, the old men leading the ANC never seemed to do anything fast enough or with enough urgency. They had too much to protect—too much invested in the status quo. In prison, he became one of those old men, but he realized that being cautious did not mean you could not be radical or bold. It's not the velocity of one's decision but the direction of it. Rapidity is not what makes one bold. In fact, taking the long view often requires being willing to change long cherished or deeply held ideas.

When he was on Robben Island, the younger prisoners often thought he was not moving fast enough or challenging the authorities forcefully enough. When he told them not to force an issue, when he argued with them for a policy that was longer-term, they would ask, "What about right now?"

"Look, you might be right for a few days, weeks and months and years," he would say, "but in the long run, you will reap something more valuable if you take a longer view."

In the long run. It is a phrase he uses often. That is the way he thinks, the distance at which his mind works best. He is not quick or facile; he likes to marinate in ideas. If everyone has a natural distance—sprinting, middle distance, long distance—Mandela is a long-distance runner, a long-distance *thinker.* And prison was a marathon.

When we were talking about an issue or a problem, he would sometimes say, "It will be better in the long run." Yes, he is an optimist, but an extremely realistic and cautious one. He is not sentimental, and he does not hope against hope. Through all those dark years, he did not believe in miracles. Miracles, if they existed, were man-made; it was hard work and discipline that helped you push things in your own direction. You could not rely on luck or divine intervention.

As soon as he became president, he knew that his overarching goal was to create a new nation. That did not mean that he did not address immediate and urgent problems; he knew that if you did not address immediate problems, you would not have the opportunity to address long-range ones. But in the main, he kept his eye on the more distant goal. And he was determined that both his short- and long-term goals should be pointing in the same direction. He often spoke of keeping "the total picture" in mind, and he almost always did. In fact, what used to nettle him were the short-term problems that were speed bumps on the way to his long-term goals. Often, those short-term problems were created by short-term thinkers, those who were guided by the headlines of the moment or the day. He was looking over the horizon.

When he emerged from prison, he saw immediately that there had been enormous advances in technology. Television had not existed in South Africa when he went to prison, let alone the twenty-four-hour cable news cycle. In his first press conference, he ducked when the camera crews took out their long, furry sound booms, which looked to him like weapons. He was amazed and delighted that you could make phone calls on a plane. But with these changes had come a radically different pace of life, and that new pace was not his pace. He did not believe that it was necessary or desirable to react to every small change in a news story. That in itself often caused problems. He knew that a rushed, short-term mistake might have long-term consequences.

Mandela thought in terms of history. History, by definition, *is* the long run. He knew you had to try to in-fluence it, but that any one individual did not make a great difference. If he were answering that old philosophical conundrum, "Does history make the man or does the man make history?" he would say that history makes the man, that great forces conspire to create great leaders. Yes, an individual has to have the right DNA and the right skills, but the moment makes the man— because only then does the man rise to meet the moment. He would say he rose to the occasion, but he knew that he did not *create* the occasion.

"He's a historical man," says Cyril Ramaphosa, the leader and activist closest to Mandela when he emerged from prison. "He was thinking way ahead of us. He has posterity in mind. How will they view what we've done? And history has absolved him. It turned out exactly as he thought it would."

Mandela believed leaders are judged in their totality, by the arc of their lives. He judged men on their entire lives and careers, not on how they reacted in one specific situation. He would often talk about the leaders who did not perform well in prison. "Ja, I know a lot of fellows, very leading chaps, who were a real disappointment in prison. You had to fight, to battle, to say let's make a stand on this issue. They wouldn't agree. 'Nel, they will kill you.'" And while he was disappointed in them, it was not a fatal defect to him because you had to judge a man by his entire life. There were men who were heroic outside of prison, but not inside it, and vice versa. Of the men who were disappointments in prison, he said, "These were men of integrity, of honor, in spite of the weaknesses which they showed." That is evidence of both his generosity and his long view. No one is as noble as the best things he has done or as venal as the worst. In his own case he knows that the good outweighs the bad, and that's ultimately what counts. But he has made decisions that he regrets. Every person is the sum of all that he or she has done.

I once asked Mandela whether he was happy. He frowned. It is the sort of question he regards as both superficial and intrusive—not a good combination. But eventually he did begin to talk. He talked about how his father had died too early and mostly a broken man. He talked about how his mother had died thinking that her son was a jailbird, perhaps a criminal. One of his great regrets is that he never helped his mother understand the struggle. He alluded to the challenges faced by his own daughters. And then he mentioned the ancient Greek writers he had read and enjoyed in prison. They took the long view. He could not recall the writer, but he said that there was the story of Croesus asking a wise man if he could be considered happy. And the wise man replied, "Count no man happy until you know his end." He agreed with that, and that is in part what made him so prudent and so cautious. Everything can change in the last chapter and you need to stay the course to prevent something untoward from happening.

Mandela is, in fact, content. He has had terrible tragedy in his life, but he now knows his own end—and he knows he has been faithful to that end, and that history will judge him kindly. Count him happy.

12

Love Makes the
Difference

W HEN IT COMES TO LOVE, Mandela is a romantic. But a pragmatic one. He had to be.

For much of his life, love was something distant, existing more in his imagination and memory than in reality. And when it was a reality, it was often a source of pain rather than solace. Yet he never gave up on the idea that love would be in his life.

The nature of apartheid-era South Africa made it impossible for him to have a public life and a private one at the same time. His public life put him in prison for twenty-seven years, where he had no private life and few consolations. Part of the diabolical nature of apartheid was to force black South Africans to separate work and family. It succeeded in Mandela's case—not because he, like so many others, was forced to work in the city while his family was in a tribal homeland, but because it was impossible to fight for freedom and live freely at the same time.

Even before he went to prison, he was forced to be a stranger to his wife and children. If you were a freedom fighter on the run, your family was a target; harassing them was the most effective way for the regime to wound you. So he stayed away from his wife and family, watching helplessly as they were hounded and tormented. Their suffering caused him to question the very bonds that should have been a source of support. Family made him more vulnerable, not less so. He was rarely able to play the role of a conventional father. Once, his older son asked him why he could never spend the night at home, and he replied that there were millions of other South African children who needed him as well. It is a terrible thing to have to say to one's own son, and in many ways, this sacrifice was the greatest pain he ever knew.

During his years in prison, love was elsewhere: in his letters, in his memory, in an imagined future. Eddie Daniels, who spent years with Mandela on Robben Island, once said to me that in prison, you had no one to console you. By this, Eddie meant both that the prisoners were a pretty unsentimental bunch and that there were no women on the Island. In my reading about Robben Island, I had come across the fact that at one time there were a number of sexual assaults in the prison. In light of this, I asked Mandela about the role sexuality played in prison. His answer was curt: "We had no avenue of sexual expression in prison." End of discussion.

But Mandela had a dream of love and family life that nourished him even when the reality was barren. During all the years he spent in prison, he cherished that dream, and when he got out, it turned out to be a mirage. Even then, he would not renounce it. Eventually, he would be rewarded, after he had almost given up hope. But it took many, many years.

⁂   ⁂   ⁂

It was Mandela's desire for romantic love, rather than his hatred of injustice, that first caused him to flee his comfortable surroundings in the countryside for the big city. It was when King Jongintaba decided that it was time to arrange marriages for his son Justice and Nelson that the two young men hatched their plot to escape to Johannesburg. It wasn't so much that they found the young women chosen for them unattractive, but that they believed devoutly that they had the right to choose themselves. It was ironic that the very education the king had made possible for Mandela had turned him against the traditional tribal ways of marriage and family. At Healdtown Methodist boarding school and Fort

183

Hare he read Jane Austen and Shakespeare's sonnets, and it was there that he came to embrace a more Western and romantic view of love than the one he experienced as a boy. His father had had four wives, whom he visited on a rotating basis. Mandela wanted love, not a maidservant.

It was in Johannesburg that he had his first romantic encounters. He developed a crush on the daughter of the family he was staying with in Alexandra Township. Her name was Didi. "She was very beautiful," he told me. She was a domestic servant—one of the few occupations available to a young black woman in the city—and had a rich boyfriend who wore double-breasted suits and a Borsalino hat and drove a fancy car. Mandela fell in love with her, but he was too insecure ever to tell her. After all, he was hardly a catch: He lived in a shack at the back of their tiny property, his English was poor, and he had one suit of clothes and little money.

One time he was invited to eat with the family, and they put a piece of chicken on his plate. As a young man from the country, he was still not used to using utensils, and rather than pick it up with his hands or struggle with a knife and fork and reveal his lack of sophistication, he chose not to eat it. Pride trumped hunger. As it did with Didi too. He said he would have asked her to marry him, but he did not want to propose to a woman who might not accept him.

When Mandela was a struggling law student, Walter Sisulu introduced him to his cousin, a quiet, unassuming young woman from the Transkei named Evelyn Mase. Mandela and Evelyn married, quickly had four children (one of whom died at nine months), and lived in a matchbox house in Soweto. Between his job, his studies, and the launch of his political career, he was mostly an absentee father and husband. Eventually, as he grew more committed to the freedom struggle, he became estranged from Evelyn. While he was having some success winning over the black masses to his cause, he was not able to do the same with his wife. She did not want to hear about politics and retreated into a different world, becoming a Jehovah's Witness who spent much of each day reading the Bible. They soon separated.

By the start of the Treason Trial in 1956, Mandela had become a successful attorney and was a man about town. He was the flashy freedom fighter and had turned into one of those fellows he used to envy: He wore double-breasted pinstriped suits, drove a big American car, and enjoyed going to restaurants. He was a ladies' man in those days and doesn't deny it. I once pointed out a picture of him from that time wearing a smart suit and holding a cigarette. I asked whether he had smoked.

"No, man," he said with a rueful smile, "I was just playing the fool."

✳ ✳ ✳

Early one morning, we were walking in the hills near Mandela's home in the Transkei, and he turned to me and asked whether or not I was married. This was unusual in that he rarely asked personal questions.

I told him I was not.

"Ah," he said.

I told him that I had recently met a South African photographer named Mary whom I was interested in. We both fell silent for a moment.

Then I asked, "How long do you have to know someone before you marry?"

"One day," he said and smiled. "One day can be long enough."

I must have given him a puzzled look because he began to elaborate. "You can love a woman at first sight," he said, "but the love can take a year or more to realize." He then went on to define different categories of attraction. "You can see a woman at a debate and be impressed by her intellect, but your emotion is not engaged. And you can see a woman and be interested in her on a superficial level." By which he meant physical attraction.

"There is no one rule," he said, "but love is the most important thing."

One day can be long enough. It was long enough, it seems, for Mandela to fall in love with his second wife. The first time he saw Winnie, he says, was from his car, while she waited at a bus stop to go to the hospital where she worked as a nurse. It was 1957. She was beautiful, he thought, and he could not get her image out of his head. A few days later, she materialized in his law office, asking about a case. It was miraculous, he felt—a bit of cosmic serendipity.

The Nelson Mandela and Winnie Madikizela of that time were very different from the ones we have come to know. She was a quiet, demure, unsophisticated young woman of twenty-two from the countryside; he was sixteen years her senior—a divorced father of three, a successful lawyer, and an admired freedom fighter. She was awed and overwhelmed by his attentions, and mostly silent in his company. He took her out for lunch (she had never had Indian food before and she drank glass after glass of water to cool her mouth), for a ride in his car, and for a walk in the countryside.

In some ways, it was a Western-style courtship, but the marriage proposal was anything but. One day, he simply told her what arrangements to make for her wedding dress. He had already consulted with a dressmaker. In fact, he admits that he never did formally ask her to marry him and she has often joked that she never got a chance to say yes.

At Mandela's wedding to Winnie, which took place during a six-day recess from the Treason Trial in 1958, her father gave a speech in which he said his daughter was marrying a "jailbird"—a man who was already married to the struggle. It was a stab at humor, but the subject was a sensitive one. To Winnie's bourgeois family, Mandela was a risky and far from ideal match for their daughter. Indeed, Nelson and Winnie never had a conventional marriage. Almost immediately after the wedding, he went underground. From that time forward, their occasional rendezvous had the character of assignations; they had to be planned in advance and the utmost security was necessary.

As her parents feared, the marriage set Winnie's life on another path entirely. Mandela recalls that when he was courting her, he was not only romancing her but politicizing her. He did his job well. Even before Mandela went to prison, Winnie had become an activist, and while he was in prison, she became the fiery "mother of the nation," a symbol of the struggle for which her husband was behind bars.

In a curious way, Mandela's love and dependence on Winnie deepened while he was in prison. His removal from her—and the world—raised her to a kind of idealized status. He fell in love all over again with the idea of their union. It was part of what kept him going—the idea that they would one day be reunited and that he could attempt to be the husband he was not able to be before. He kept a portrait of her in his cell, and he once wrote to her: "Your beautiful photo still stands about two feet above my left shoulder as I write this note. I dust it carefully every morning, for to do so gives me the pleasant feeling that I'm caressing you as in the old days. I even touch your nose with mine to capture the electric current that used to flush through my blood whenever I did so."

He looked forward to her visits for months and was crushed when she could not come or when prison authorities canceled them. He became far more expressive to her in letters than he had ever been in person, even though these letters were read and sometimes censored by the prison authorities. In August of 1970, at a particularly difficult time—Winnie herself was in prison and he was uncertain who was looking after their daughters—he ached with pain and told her so in their correspondence:

> The number of miseries we have harvested from the heartbreaking frustrations of the last 15 months are not likely to fade away easily from the mind. I feel as if I have been soaked in gall, every part of me, my flesh

from body and soul, so bitter I am to be
completely powerless to help you in . . . [the]
ordeals you are going through. . . . if only we
could meet; if I could be on your side &
squeeze you, or if I could but catch a glimpse
of your outline through the thick wire netting
that would inevitably separate us. Physical suffering is nothing compared to the trampling
down of these tender bonds of affection.

The one thing that could make him lose his temper
was an insult to his wife. The guards knew this and
would occasionally leave press clippings on his bed
about Winnie being imprisoned or linked to other men.
To the authorities, Winnie and his family were his
Achilles' heel. Mandela recalled for me how he had almost assaulted a guard who had said something offen-
sive about Winnie. "There was a head of prison . . . who
said something uncomplimentary about Winnie, and of
course, I was very annoyed and lost my temper and I
told him a few regrettable things and they charged me
for that. . . . I almost clipped the fellow. In fact I
checked myself as I was going for him, and let out
steam by swearing at him. I think I used very strong
language."

These trials and setbacks might easily have made

Mandela cynical about love and inured to its absence. But the dream of intimacy is a potent one, and as he got older Mandela became even more of a romantic.

Yet there was no storybook ending to his marriage to Winnie. When he emerged from prison, they were not able to pick up where they had left off many years earlier. To the outside world, Winnie appeared to be the strong and loyal wife. But behind the scenes, there was great tension. As one of Mandela's aides told me, "No one expected Winnie to be faithful for twenty-seven years. She's a human being too."

Nobody wanted to tell the old man. But he began to ask his friends, and he was profoundly wounded to learn the truth of Winnie's behavior. As his confidante said to me about that time, "She humiliated him. And he loves that woman. She thought he would never leave her, but he had to, for the organization." She was undermining the freedom struggle *and* their marriage: Mandela might have tolerated one, but he could not tolerate both.

By the time I started working with Mandela, he was already separated from Winnie. She was a difficult topic of conversation, and I found that Mandela was most at ease in talking about Winnie in the past—and least comfortable talking about her in the present. One day in January, when he was discussing the time he had been in prison, he spoke about her in a full-throated way. She

had had it worse than he had, he said. She had been ha-
rassed and imprisoned by the authorities, and all the
while she still had to look after the children, which he
did not. The stresses of being outside of prison could be
greater, he said, than the stresses of being inside. At one
point she had spent more than a year in solitary confinement, while he had spent only a handful of nights in
solitary.

One Sunday, we talked in the sunny living room of
his house in Houghton in the Johannesburg suburbs.
He had his stockinged feet up on an ottoman in front
of his easy chair and we were about to begin. At that
moment, his housekeeper, Miriam, walked in with the
Sunday papers and his eyes lit up. Mandela loves newspapers. For years and years, he was deprived of papers
on Robben Island, so even today a newspaper seems to
him like a rare and precious gift. He asked me if I
minded if he glanced through them before we started.
A few minutes later, he started chuckling. There was a
headline that said WINNIE FOR PRESIDENT and an arti-
cle about some remarks that Winnie had made at the
funeral of anti-apartheid campaigner Helen Joseph, in
which she had criticized the ANC, and by implication
Mandela, for being too cozy with the government.

I asked whether he was surprised by what she
had said.

"I have been with Comrade Winnie since 1958," he said, in a tone mixing fondness and exasperation. "Nothing that she does surprises me. She has taken everything that the regime has given her." He paused, then added, "But to make a statement that is likely to divide the organization at a critical moment is something that one doesn't expect, no matter how bitter she may be."

As the two comments reveal, Mandela's feelings about Winnie remain mixed, and they are seasoned with disappointment. He is nostalgic about the old days and realistic about the present. For a long time, a kind of armed truce existed between the two in which they maintained a stiff formality. But in recent years, they have resumed a warm friendship.

※　　※　　※

Over the months, Mandela got to know my friend Mary. It turned out that they had met before, on the day of his release. She worked for the French photo agency Agence France-Presse, and he remembered the elegant red-haired photographer who had shot him as he walked out of prison. In the beginning, when Mary would pick me up after I returned from a trip with Mandela, he would tease her: "You mustn't take Richard away from us." But within a couple of months, he said to me, "You know, you must marry her." She later told me that on another occasion, he had taken her aside, held her hand, and said, "You must marry Richard. I will give you my blessing." It was not an order, of course, but he had become a kind of godfather to our relationship. It was because of him that we met and we both felt he had a special insight into our relationship. At some level, I felt he was articulating something I felt but had not yet expressed. Later, I happily discovered that Mary felt the same way. But he was not nearly as reserved or as tentative as we were. Perhaps that came from his feeling that he had lost many years and much happiness and did not want us to lose any.

It was always obvious that Mandela enjoys the company of women. He is more relaxed and unguarded with women than men—happier, more carefree. I saw it with Mary; when she was with us he was also more candid, more willing to show a vulnerable side. He is also flirtatious, but in a gallant, old world, grandfatherly way.

In 1993 and 1994, he was often accompanied by a young Japanese acupuncturist named Chikako. He had met her on a trip to Japan when he was having trouble with his legs. His close aide, Barbara Masekela, had recommended that he have acupuncture for his swollen legs.

"You know I was very reluctant to have this sort of

treatment," he says. "Barbara was very insistent. It was explained to me that this was a traditional method of healing that had been scientifically verified. And then I learned that it was a woman, and a young woman. I am used to male doctors, older male doctors. You know, I didn't like the idea of a young woman coming up to my hotel room. I finally agreed when Barbara said that she would remain in the room."

His apprehension disappeared when he met Chikako. She was a tiny sprite of a woman with a shy smile and a gentle manner. She had trained as a classical acupuncturist and she later spent months treating him in South Africa. She called him "Tata" (the Xhosa word for father), was devoted to him, and went with him to the Transkei and on foreign trips. He treated her like a granddaughter.

Mandela enjoyed teasing her. One day the three of us were walking in the Transkei and she asked him whether his knee was bothering him. He smiled and said no. "When you are near me," he said, "I feel no pain whatsoever. It is only when you go away that I feel any pain." She bowed her head and smiled.

Mandela seemed to always have a sixth sense about others' loneliness. He saw that Chikako was mostly by herself when she was not with him and probably homesick. Once, we were all together on New Year's Eve

1993, at a hotel in Durban. We had ended up in a rather cheesy disco with a band playing pop music from the seventies and eighties—songs the rest of us had heard hundreds of times but that Mandela was probably hearing for the first time. He noticed that she was bopping her head, and he caught my attention and gave the universal signal of a father to a son saying, ask your younger sister to dance. I did, and when we came back, he said to me, "Well done."

Another morning, Mandela and I were having breakfast in his dining room and Chikako walked by. He called out, "Come, sit down here, man." (He used "man" with men and women.) He patted the chair next to him and said, "Chikako is the only one who loves me." I said millions of people loved him. He smiled and said, "Yes, but Chikako loves me from up close, and those people love me from a distance." She laughed along with him, but it was a revealing comment. Mandela did feel loved abstractly, but he had few people with whom he was intimate. Those who should have been closest to him— Winnie, some of his children—were distant or estranged. He was lonely and felt that he had once again become a kind of prisoner—this time isolated by celebrity and power.

It was during that same time that Mandela was

courting the woman who would help make up for those lost years. Graça Machel was the widow of Samora Machel, the revolutionary leader of Mozambique who died in a plane crash in 1986. She was an esteemed political figure in Mozambique, a crusader for the poor and disenfranchised. Then forty-eight, she was warm and stable. He had first met her in 1990, a few months after his release, when he visited Mozambique, and they had stayed in touch. After his official separation from Winnie in 1992, he began to court her. Even though they were falling in love, she was reluctant to marry. Instead, she accompanied him on trips and he would visit her in Mozambique. In 1993 and 1994, their relationship was still a secret, but he told me of his affection for her. I was often with him when he was on the phone with her, and he would tell her to pack a sweater if the weather was cool or to bring an umbrella if it was rainy.

Mandela divorced Winnie in 1996, and in 1998 he went public with his romance. "I'm in love with a remarkable lady," he said on television. "I don't regret the reverses and setbacks because late in my life I am blooming like a flower, because of the love and support she has given me."

As Graça said after they married on Mandela's eightieth birthday in 1998, "He can love very deeply, but he tries to control it very well in his public appearance. In private, he can allow himself to be a human being. He likes people to know he is happy."

Throughout his life, in the calculus between love and duty, duty almost always won out. There is little room for love in the life of a revolutionary and a prisoner. But Mandela never gave up on love, not even when it was postponed or inaccessible. If anything, his belief in the power of love grew stronger while he was in prison. He once said to me, "When you love a woman, you don't see her faults. The love is everything. You don't pay attention to the things others may find wrong with her. You just love her."

That is the way he was. Finally, at the age of eighty, he found that love and happiness with Graça Machel. It was the happy ending he had been seeking for half a century.

13

Quitting Is
Leading Too

I N MANY WAYS, Mandela's greatest act of leadership
was the renunciation of it.

When he became the first democratically elected
president of a free South Africa, he probably could have
stayed president for life if he had wanted to. He would
certainly have been elected by acclamation to a second
five-year term. But he knew his real job was, as Cyril
Ramaphosa put it, "to set the course, not steer the ship."
So, in April 1995, only a year into his first term, he remarked that in 1999 he would be eighty years old and
that "an octogenarian shouldn't be meddling in politics."
When asked if he would stand for a second term, he
replied, "Definitely not." And he did not. That was a
defining act of leadership.

Mandela was not the first political prisoner to become president of an African nation. In fact, he was part
of a twentieth-century tradition. There was Kenyatta in
Kenya, Nkrumah in Ghana, Mugabe in Zimbabwe.
What Africa had rarely experienced was a president who

left office voluntarily—either constitutionally or by the will of the people. Most had left horizontally or at the barrel of an AK-47. Mandela's contemporary, President Robert Mugabe of Zimbabwe, is still clutching at power after destroying his own country.

Mandela was determined to show not only that Africans could govern themselves, but that Africa could be a continent of constitutional democracies. He was in many ways the African mirror of George Washington, who decided to serve two terms as the first U.S. president and then voluntarily went back to being a private citizen. Washington's decision to forgo the possibility of lifelong office (which many advocated) set the template for the American presidency. Like Washington, Mandela understood that his footsteps would be the first ones in the sand and that others would follow. Mandela knew that his own example would be more enduring, more influential, than any single policy he would ever enact.

When he finally did leave office, he believed that he should truly retire, that he should be like the Roman leader Cincinnatus, who went back to his farm and lived a quiet life. Mandela did not particularly want a quiet life—he still loved the limelight—but he understood that he could not voluntarily leave office and have people think he still secretly yearned to be president. When you leave the stage, you can't keep poking your head around the curtain. For the first few years, he was resolute about not commenting on his successor's policies. He understood that he had set the course; now it was time for others to steer the ship.

＃　　＃　　＃

Mandela knows that it doesn't pay to fight over every issue, and that sometimes it's best to call it quits. There are situations in which we might do better to save our capital. On Robben Island, the prisoners were constantly debating one another. They could debate anything under the sun, but there were a few set topics: whether the Communist Party and the ANC were one, whether a future democratic government of South Africa should include the Afrikaner-dominated National Party, and perhaps the most contentious topic (and certainly the most amusing one): whether the tiger was indigenous to Africa. In fact, there are no tigers in Africa; the tiger is indigenous to India and Asia. Over the years, however, there were many prisoners who were convinced that Africa was the home of the tiger, and they argued their case passionately. There was one particular prisoner who was vociferous on this subject, and one day Mandela told him that it was a simple fact that there were no tigers in Africa. The prisoner blew up, and Mandela's reaction was not to fight but to cede the argument—"very well," he said—and wait. And wait he did, until a few years later, a prisoner arrived who had studied zoology and traveled around the world. Of course, the new arrival said, the tiger is not native to Africa. That satisfied everyone—even the adamant prisoner. Mandela did not even gloat.

＊　　＊　　＊

Mandela has always been stubborn. Everyone testifies to this, from his closest colleagues on the Island to his wife, Graça Machel. When he makes up his mind, it is hard for anyone to change it. But change it he does, particularly when faced with evidence that not changing his mind will yield negative consequences. He will fight and argue and attempt to persuade, but the moment he realizes that his is not the practical or wise choice, he will simply relent—and that will be that.

One day, Mandela asked me if I knew of any countries where the voting age was under eighteen. I knew why he was asking. The election was coming up, and half of the South African population was under the age of eighteen—the lion's share of them young black South Africans who would vote for his party, the African National Congress, if given the chance.

I did some research and supplied him with what turned out to be a not-very-distinguished list: Cuba, Nicaragua, North Korea, Indonesia, and Iran. Nevertheless, he was pleased, and said, "Very good, very good," his highest praise. Two weeks later, he went on South African television and proposed that the voting age be lowered to fourteen. There was an immediate outcry in the media and in his own party. People thought the idea was daft, and many used much less generous words than that.

A few weeks later, I teased him by saying that his idea had not exactly been met with universal acclaim. He frowned, tipped his head back, and said he would carry the day. Ultimately, the opposition proved too strong. "He tried to sell us the idea," recalls Ramaphosa, who was on the National Executive Committee, "but he was the only [supporter]. And he had to face the reality that it would not win the day. He accepted it with great humility. He doesn't sulk."

When Mandela reverses himself, you would never know he had ever felt differently. He goes over to the other side and embraces it with the zeal of the newly converted. He will even laugh at how he once fought for the opposition. Years afterward, he would wink at me whenever the issue of the fourteen-year-old vote came up. He understands that yielding can be a kind of victory, too—that surrendering means that you are going over to the winning side. Then you, too, can claim victory.

14

It's Always Both

N ELSON MANDELA IS COMFORTABLE with contradictions. Even his own. When I was with him, I sometimes thought of the lines from Walt Whitman's "Song of Myself":

Do I contradict myself?
Very well then I contradict myself,
(I am large, I contain multitudes.)

He *is* large. He does contain multitudes. And he often contradicts himself. He understands that consistency for its own sake is a false virtue, and that inconsistency is not automatically a flaw. He knows that humans are complex creatures and that people have a myriad of motives.

During an interview, I once asked Mandela: Did you embrace the armed struggle because you thought nonviolence would never defeat apartheid or because it was the only way to keep the ANC from splintering apart? We had been working together for about a month, and we were still getting used to each other. In the early weeks of our conversations, Mandela was quite formal and would answer my sometimes cumbersome questions as though he were at a press conference, launching into stiff and predictable answers. As we became more comfortable with each other, he would treat my questions as a jumping-off point to tell stories or make a larger point. But at this time in our relationship, we fell somewhere in between. Normally, he would consider a question for a moment, and then look off into the distance as he began unspooling his answer. This time, however, he fixed me with a look that seemed to combine perplexity and annoyance.

And then he said, "Richard, why not both?"

Why not both?

I often posed questions in that binary manner: Was something this way or that? Was the reason A or B? Yes/no? Early on, I saw that this frustrated him, because for Mandela the answer is almost always both. It's never as simple as yes or no. He knows that the reason behind any action is rarely clear. There are no simple answers to most difficult questions. All explanations may be true. Every problem has many causes, not just one. That is the way Nelson Mandela sees the world.

He once recited for me the parable of the young Xhosa man who left his small village to search for a wife. He spent years traveling all around the world looking for the perfect woman, but did not find her. Eventually he came back to the village without a bride, and on his way in saw a woman and said, "Ah, I have found my wife." It turns out, Mandela said, that she had lived in the hut next door to his all her life. I asked, "Is the moral of the story that you don't need to wander far and wide to find what you are looking for because it is right in front of you? Or is it that sometimes you must have wide experience and knowledge in order to appreciate those things that are closest and most familiar to you?"

He thought about this for a moment, nodded, and then said, "There is no one interpretation. Both may be correct."

＃　　＃　　＃

When Mandela emerged from prison, people assumed he saw the world in black and white. After all, he had sacrificed most of his adult life to a simple and clear ideal. He had righteousness on his side, as well as the world's popular opinion. Apartheid had few if any defenders. But the seventy-one-year-old man who emerged from prison turned out to be far more subtle than people anticipated. He understood white fears and black frustrations; he appreciated the pull of tribalism and the power of modernism; he saw the appeal of nationalization and the allure of the free market; he understood the Afrikaner's love of rugby and the freedom fighter's abhorrence of it. He almost always saw both sides of every issue, and his default position was to find some course in between, some way of reconciling both sides. In part this came from his deep-seated need to persuade and win people over, but mostly it came from having a nonideological view of the world and an appreciation for the intricate spider's web of human motives.

I saw the subtlety of his understanding in the way that he treated his colleagues—he always saw a mixture of motives, good and bad, honorable and ignoble. I saw it in the way he looked at issues—knowing that neither side had an exclusive claim on virtue or correctness. I remember him telling me about the struggle over food on the Island. Indian and Colored prisoners had a slightly better diet with more meat. The African prisoners protested that the diet should be the same, and it was easy to understand their point of view. But he also took the trouble to talk to the Indian and Colored prisoners, who were concerned that their diet would be worsened in the interest of a "false equality." Ultimately, he persuaded the authorities to provide everyone with the better diet. He saw all sides, talked to all sides, and tried to reconcile all sides.

Of course, it is not always possible to make everyone happy. At times there were painful situations in which he could see both sides but had to accede to one of them. He understood the traditional African reticence about AIDS and HIV, but he knew that it was a mistake not to get antiretroviral drugs for the millions who were suffering in his country. He wanted Cyril Ramaphosa as his successor, but he understood why his closest colleagues preferred Thabo Mbeki. And when it came to divorcing Winnie, perhaps the most painful personal decision of his life, he still saw much that was good in her but knew what he had to do. It was precisely because he was able to hold both good and bad in his mind at once—the memory of what he had loved best in her and the knowledge that she was hurting him—that the decision was so excruciating for him.

In his negotiations for the country's first government, he made many fundamental compromises in order to come to an agreement. Though many of his colleagues staunchly opposed it, he gave the National Party the right to keep their civil service jobs, and he gave them a unity government, in which Mr. de Klerk was vice president. But he could see the Nationalists' side, and he knew that the overarching goal was what was important. Yes, there were some principles that were nonnegotiable—one-person, one-vote, universal democracy—but after that, most things were in shades of gray.

Shades of gray are not easy to articulate. Black-and-white is seductive because it is simple and absolute. It appears clear and decisive. Because of that, we will often gravitate toward yes or no answers when a "both" or a "maybe" is closer to the truth. Some people will choose a categorical yes or no simply because they think it appears strong. But if we cultivate the habit of considering both—or even several—sides of a question, as Mandela did, of holding both good and bad in our minds, we may see solutions that would not otherwise have occurred to us. This way of thinking is demanding. Even if we remain wedded to our point of view, it requires us to put ourselves in the shoes of those with whom we disagree. That takes an effort of will, and it requires empathy and imagination. But the reward, as we can see in the case of Mandela, is something that can fairly be described as wisdom.

Wandsworth Libraries
Self service

Wandsworth

Monday, Sept 17, 2012 - 11:50

Borrower number: ****4568

You have borrowed 1 item

Title	Due	Fee
Mandela's way: lessons in life	08/10/12	None

You have 2 other items on loan

Title	Due
Maisy's train	04/10/12
Disney Mini Board Books - Princess - Cinderella:	04/10/12

Amount owing: NONE

Please note: This does not include any charges for overdue items which have not yet been returned

Thank you for using this service

15

Find Your Own
Garden

E VEN ON A REMOTE but beautiful island, Mandela needed a place apart. A place where he could lose himself to find himself.

The early years on Robben Island were bleak. The warders were coarse and abusive. The work was back-breaking. And the prisoners were permitted only one visitor and a single letter every six months. For Mandela, the outside world appeared equally harsh. His eldest son was killed in a car crash. Winnie was under constant threat. The ANC was in exile. And the apartheid government had consolidated its power.

So, in the early 1970s, amid all these troubles, Nelson Mandela decided to plant a garden.

This sounds easier than it was. First, he had to ask permission from the prison authorities, who were suspicious of the most innocent request. Even a simple request could take months. He explained that he wanted to supplement his diet and that of his colleagues with fresh vegetables, and he prepared a campaign to persuade the authorities to accede to his request. Letters went back and forth within the prison bureaucracy. Memos were written. Lawyers were consulted. Finally, in the dirt courtyard just in front of the row of prisoners' cells, Mandela was permitted to plant a small, narrow garden.

The ground was dry and rocky and inhospitable. The garden was approximately thirty-five feet long and a yard wide and ran parallel to the row of single cells. Guards were positioned to watch him dig and plant.

At first he used his hands, but he soon acquired some tools: a shovel, a rake. He asked family and friends to send him seeds. While other men were playing checkers or reading or talking in the courtyard, Mandela tended his garden. The other prisoners smiled at the old man and his garden. He was very proud of it.

"The soil was not very good," he told me, "but I managed, you know, to produce some good harvests."

He grew tomatoes, onions, chilies, spinach. He was permitted to give the vegetables to the kitchen to be mixed into the prisoners' regular diet of cornmeal and the occasional piece of meat. For the first few years, the prison officials remained skeptical of Mandela and his garden. They suspected that he had some nefarious motive that they could not divine. Mandela was amused by their reaction.

"You know there are graves all over Robben Island,"

he told me one morning. "When I was digging my garden in the courtyard, I found many bones. I would take these bones, break them up a bit, and then put them in the sun to dry, so that I could grind them up for fertilizer for my garden. One day, the CO [commanding officer], who was a very nervous chap, came by and saw the bones and said to one of my comrades, 'What are those bones? What is Mandela doing with them?' Quite nervous, you know. The fellow shrugged his shoulders and said he didn't know. And then he came to me and said, 'Mandela, what are you doing with those bones?' I told him, 'I am using them for fertilizer; grinding them up and using them for fertilizer.' The CO seemed skeptical. 'No,' I said, 'bones are a well-known, well-established fertilizer.' But the CO still seemed to have reservations and said, 'Mandela, from now on, we will buy you fertilizer in town. You simply tell us what you need and how much and we will get it for you. But no more digging up bones.' I later found out that he thought I was trying to embarrass the prison service and government by digging up old bones and saying that prisoners had been secretly buried on Robben Island."

Mandela began to write about his garden in letters to Winnie and others. He related how his plants and vegetables were doing as though they were his children. He talked about the seasons and the soil and his harvest.

Some people may have suspected that he was talking metaphorically, but he was simply writing about what gave him pleasure. By the late 1970s, as the Island began to become a bit less oppressive, Mandela would give vegetables to the guards for their families and he was allowed to plant a second garden outside the courtyard. Soon the warders were supplying him with seeds and he was supplying them with produce.

During the time we worked together, I made a trip to Cape Town to see Robben Island. At our next session after my visit, I told Mandela I'd been to the Island. His first question to me was not whether I had seen his cell or the lime quarry or the solitary confinement block. It was, "Did they show you where my garden was?"

In fact, they hadn't. The guards who had taken me around had not been on the Island when Mandela had been there. They didn't even know about the garden. I had seen everything else, but the garden was gone. Mandela was disappointed.

On Robben Island, where there were few pleasures, Mandela's garden had become his own private island. It quieted his mind. It distracted him from his constant worries about the outside world, his family, and the freedom struggle. While so much was withering outside, his garden was thriving. Mandela has always had great powers of concentration, and the other prisoners noted how absorbed he was when he was gardening. He got lost in it. "He loved that garden," Ahmed Kathrada told me.

\#   \#   \#

It was in 1982, when Mandela was transferred to Pollsmoor Prison on the mainland, that he became even more serious about gardening. He and three fellow prisoners were given a spacious room on the third floor of the prison. As the only prisoners on the floor, they had access to a large terrace that was open to the sky. It was there that Mandela constructed an impressive garden using thirty-two forty-four-gallon oil drums that had been sliced in half and filled with soil. He grew tomatoes, onions, eggplant, strawberries, spinach, cabbage, broccoli, beetroot, lettuce, and cauliflower. He worked on the garden for two hours every morning after his exercises, and then again in the afternoon. It became more than just an avocation. It was time out of mind, where he could do something life affirming and creative.

"Now, I had very good soil," he recalled to me one day, "which we brought from outside the prison and we got very good manure and, oh, how it thrived!" When

Mandela talked about this garden his whole face became sunny.

He studied gardening. He ordered books on agriculture and horticulture that he paid for himself. He once spent half an hour telling me about the different fertilizers that he used, explaining for example that pigeon manure "is very dangerous, it's very strong. You have to be very careful. Powder it, put it in water, and make sure that it is very thin." He was as commanding in talking about fertilizers as he was about politics.

He was rueful in recalling that he could not grow peanuts. "I must confess my knowledge of how to grow peanuts was not so good. They never thrived." But he recalled with pride how the commanding officer once asked the warders to get him a cutting of Mandela's spinach because the plants had grown so tall. "I took a lot of pride in that garden. On Sunday, I used to supply the whole kitchen staff with vegetables; yes, every Sunday."

In 1985, he was transported to Cape Town for prostate surgery, and when he came back, he was put on the first floor, separated from his colleagues. It was the end of the garden, and he mourned the loss for months afterward.

In a world where he had no privacy and very few possessions, the garden had been a bit of land that was entirely his. In a world that he could not control, that defied and punished him, that seemed hostile to his values and his dreams, it had been a place of beauty and regularity and renewal. Effort was rewarded. The seasons changed in regular order. Seeds turned into plants. Stalks rose. Leaves sprouted.

In cultivating his garden, Mandela was also renewing a cherished memory from his childhood. In his prison diary, he recalls being taken to Mqhekezweni, the Great Place, after his father died, and seeing the king's garden "in the shade of two gum trees. . . . There were peach trees and maize in the front garden, and a larger garden at the back that had apple trees, maize, a vegetable and flower strip, and a wattle patch." He was in awe of that garden.

He would occasionally use garden metaphors when we talked. Men, he said, could be cultivated like plants. He once said that each of us should cultivate our own garden, but he also made it clear that, unlike Voltaire's Candide, he did not think we should remove ourselves from life in order to do it. For Mandela, his life was in service to others, and the garden was a respite from the turmoil and storms of the world. In that way, it helped him do his main work. It was not a place of retreat but of renewal.

Samuel Johnson once said there was nothing more

relaxing than concentrating on a pleasant task that engages the mind but does not tax it too much. For Johnson, that was a chemistry set; for Mandela, it was a garden. For the rest of us, it might be something else entirely. The main thing is that each of us needs something away from the world that gives us pleasure and satisfaction, a place apart.

As Mandela once said to me, "You must find your own garden."

Mandela's Gift

YES, I TOOK MANDELA'S ADVICE—Mary and I were married in 1994. Three years later, on Christmas Eve, we called him to say that Mary was pregnant. He was delighted. Hoping for a laugh, I told him that if it was a boy, we'd name him Rolihlahla. Rolihlahla, as only a few people know, is Mandela's real first name. It means Tree Shaker in Xhosa. With a trilled *r* at the beginning and two fricative sounds at the end, it's even more difficult to pronounce than it is to spell. I've never heard anyone call him by that name and he never uses it, so I meant it as a kind of inside joke. But he did not laugh. There was silence. Had I garbled the pronunciation? Did he think it was presumptuous for a white American to make a joke about his name? After a pause, he said he'd like to speak to Mary. I handed her the phone, and the moment after she said hello, I could hear his great foghorn of a voice say, "I cannot wait to see you—and the little Rolihlahla!"

A few months later, when we were in the hospital

after our first son was born, the rather stern nurse brought around her clipboard for us to write down his name. We looked at each other and remembered that Christmas phone call. No, we couldn't really do it as his first name. . . . Then, in block letters in a firm hand, I wrote GABRIEL ROLIHLAHLA STENGEL.

My sons are still young, but they have each met their namesake a number of times. Our younger boy, Anton, has demanded his own Mandela middle name, and we have told him that it is Madiba, which is Mandela's clan name and what many friends call him. Do they fully understand who Nelson Mandela is, what he stands for, and what role he has played in their own lives? They do not. To them, he is a smiling white-haired old man who embraces them, holds their hands, and asks them what sports they like and what they had for breakfast. But someday they will know. They will know who he is, what he has accomplished, and that he is part of what binds us together as a family. They will know that they have a special golden thread that connects them to this heroic, historical figure and the values he championed. I devoutly hope that it will make them better men and that it is a gift they will somehow try to repay.

When I imagine Mandela's legacy to my sons, I recall that heartbreaking exchange Mandela had with his first son, who once asked his father why he could never spend the night with the family. Because there were millions of other children who needed him, Mandela answered. As difficult and even harsh as that might sound, it was the simple and yet terrible calculation that Mandela had made. One of the things Mandela sought through his own sacrifice was that someday other fathers and mothers would not have to say those same words to their sons and daughters; that his son might inherit a free nation where he would not have to fight for the freedom that should have been his birthright. In a larger way, Mandela wants there to be a thread between his life, his values, his achievements, and everyone who comes after him. As unique as he might be, he would tell you that he is part of a long chain of leadership—a continuum of those who came before us and those who will succeed us, a great and powerful chain of those fighting to enlarge human freedom.

In Mandela's case, he steeped himself in models of leadership from the time he was a boy. From the king who raised him, he learned the importance of listening and guiding rather than ruling by fiat. He sat at the king's feet, listened to the stories of ancient Xhosa chiefs who fought for their people, and saw himself as the heir to a long tradition of African heroes. From the English headmasters at his schools, he learned the importance of study and honor and discipline. While at Fort Hare, he listened to Winston Churchill's stirring wartime speeches and saw how a leader can inspire a nation. From Walter Sisulu, his first mentor in Johannesburg, he learned how to be pragmatic and realistic in pursuit of his goals. From his law partner and friend Oliver Tambo, he learned to rein in his emotions, to be patient and not react too quickly. On the one trip he took outside South Africa before he was confined to prison for decades, he was impressed by Tanzanian president Julius Nyerere's presentation of himself as a man of the people, with a modest house and small car. In Addis Ababa, he was struck by Haile Selassie's regal dignity and his fanciful uniforms. On Robben Island, he became his own teacher in many ways, but from his lifelong friend Sisulu (the other prisoners referred to Walter as Allah, because he was so wise), he learned how to include other viewpoints, make peace with rivals, and find consensus.

Even after emerging from prison and becoming South Africa's first democratically elected president, he continued to learn from other leaders. He told me how pleased and honored he was that the first President George Bush included him in his rounds of calls to world leaders, and he admired his generosity. He was greatly taken by Bill Clinton's warmth and energy and youthfulness, and saw that a more informal style of leadership than his own could be highly effective. From

Tony Blair, he saw how important it was for a leader to be able to explain ideas and policies to the people, even when the voters did not agree with them.

The chain of leadership is particularly important to Mandela because of the African concept of *ubuntu*—what Westerners would call brotherhood. This idea, which I mentioned in Chapter 4, is vital to understanding how Mandela thinks and sees himself. The word comes from a Zulu proverb, *Umuntu ngumuntu ngabantu*, which is often translated as, "A person is a person through other people." The idea is that we do nothing entirely on our own, a concept that is poles apart from the notion of individualism that has characterized the West since the Renaissance. Ubuntu sees people less as individuals than as part of an infinitely complex web of other human beings. It is the idea that we are all bound up with one another, that *me* is always subordinate to *we,* that no man is an island.

Mandela would sometimes talk about his grandchildren and I'd say, "But so-and-so is not the child of one of your children." He would smile and shake his head and say, "In our culture, the children of our relatives are all grandchildren." Mandela was amused by the literalness of Western family trees. In his view, we are all branches of the same great family tree. That is ubuntu.

Although we might all have some connection to

Mandela, he also stands alone and outside of us, an incarnation of something larger than ourselves, an embodiment of the best of humankind. His experience is both singular and universal. He moves us because he is the modern-day example of the archetypal hero, the man who is plucked out of nowhere, takes on a momentous challenge, suffers great trials and tragedy and almost fails, and then is resurrected and achieves harmony. It is the same narrative we see with Buddha, Moses, Muhammad, and Jesus. Mandela's life has the same arc and a similar resonance.

※　※　※

Like those other great figures, Mandela inspires a sense of trust. Trust is a foundation of leadership. We trust that a leader is honest, able, and has a vision of where to go. But trust operates on an even deeper level. We trust that a leader is who he appears to be, that the public person and the private one are the same. In his case, Nelson Mandela is the man he seems to be. The values that he espouses in public are the values he practices in private. In all the times we were together, he never leaned forward to say, "Well, off the record, so-and-so is a nasty piece of work." He contains many contradictions, but few hypocrisies.

Of course that does not mean he cannot disappoint you, or even sometimes be petty. He will sometimes not confront things or not fulfill promises. He knows that earnestness and humility might be public virtues, but they are not necessarily private ones. He has human appetites and does not hide them, though he does his best to tamp them down. He is great because he has triumphed over his flaws, not because he does not have them.

I once asked him whether he had been surprised by how much he was lionized when he emerged from prison, his face on millions of posters and T-shirts. I teased him that he had become a living legend.

"No-o-o," he said, almost recoiling. "I don't think it is healthy for people to think of you as a messiah. In that case, they will only be disappointed. They should know that their leaders are made of flesh and blood, that they are human. I want them to think that of me. If they think you are a savior, their expectations are far too high. Let them think of you as a hero, yes, but not a legend."

The world has not only lionized Mandela. It has also sentimentalized him, turning him into a kind of black Santa Claus, the benign old man who made unimaginable sacrifices for a moral cause, a smiling symbol of pure goodness. But hero or not, he is no angel. He has made many, many hard decisions in his life—decisions that may have been wrong or unfair, decisions that have hurt and wounded people, even cost them their lives. He knows that leadership often means having to choose between two bad options and that good men have to make decisions that have bad consequences.

At the same time, making hard decisions does not have to mean violating first principles. As he would say, you must reflect the goal in the way you seek it. He would sometimes quote Gandhi: "Be the change that you seek." Mandela was tolerant of everything but intolerance. He would never discriminate in his goal to end discrimination. A noble goal should not be pursued by ignoble means. Practical ones, yes. Venal ones, no.

It is that very practicality—and not only humility—that led Mandela to reject being viewed as a savior. Such talk sets the bar too high. Ultimately, he did not want to overpromise and underdeliver—that is death for a politician and certainly a messiah.

So, I asked him, what is the difference then between a legend and a hero? "Ah, you know, there are very few legends. Legends are very rare; something that has not been seen. But there are thousands of heroes in South Africa today. A hero is a man who believes in something, who is courageous, who may risk his own life for the good of the community." Mandela knows he has been a hero, but even a hero stands on the shoulders of others. There were thousands of men and women who risked their lives so he could risk his; thousands of men and women who whose unknown and unremembered acts of courage allowed him to demonstrate his.

Courage is rooted in the here and now. Mandela is a materialist in the philosophical sense. He distrusts anything he cannot touch and for years avoided any reference to or reliance on a higher power. He relied on his comrades, not a distant deity. He did not pray; he pondered and then acted. To those who would say that everything happens for a reason, he would reply that *we* are the reason and we are the ones who make things happen. There is no destiny that shapes our end; we shape it ourselves.

\# \# \#

It has become a cliché for leaders to say they have no regrets. It is as though admitting to regrets is evidence of weakness. Mandela has plenty of regrets. On the big issues, he believes he chose the right course, but he knows he has made many wrong turns along the way. His sadness comes from wondering about the paths not taken, about whether the sacrifice of his private life was worth it. He would ultimately say yes, but that doesn't help the pain.

After the Chris Hani assassination I went with Mandela to Hani's house, where he met with Hani's widow. After speaking to her alone, he addressed the twenty or so people who were there. His empathy for Mrs. Hani was palpable. She was a very strong woman, he said, "but her wounds are invisible to the eye. Unseen wounds are very painful, even more painful than the wounds you can see." It was clear to me that he was talking about himself too.

We held our last official interview on a weekend morning at his house in Houghton. I was always trying to push him toward being more poetic and philosophical, and he almost always eschewed it. On this final day, I tried to get him to be a little more introspective, and, as usual, he offered practical, policy-oriented answers to all my questions. But toward the end, after all my prodding, he paused, looked out the window, and said, "Men come and men go. I have come and I will go when my time comes." Even his eloquence is down to earth.

When our time was up, he stood and I went to shake his hand. I knew I might not see him again for some time, and that we had arrived at the end of an intensely intimate journey, and I put my other arm around his shoulder. Mandela is not a physically demonstrative person, but after the briefest of moments, he put his arm around mine and drew me closer into an embrace. At that point, I could not help it and I hugged him fiercely. I could feel the back of his head against mine and his arm on my back. I know he could feel my emotion and I did my best to hold back my tears. Even at seventy-five, he stood tall and straight and firm. At that moment, I could not help but think of Eddie Daniels, the five-foot-three prisoner on Robben Island, who had said that when he was really despondent, if he could just see Mandela, touch him, embrace him, it was enough to console him, to revive him, to make him want to live again. I thought of the hundreds, perhaps thousands, of men over the decades, men in dire and terrible circumstances, men in fear and despair, men facing pain and even death who had clutched him for comfort and strength. He understood this and let me hold him.

After a long moment he said all right, and we let go, and I stood back and watched him as he slowly made his way upstairs.

※　※　※

I have seen Mandela many times in the years since we worked together, but I would be a liar if I said that I ever shared that same intimacy with him again or that I didn't yearn to do so. In fact, I became like one of those hundreds of men who lived side by side with him under the most trying and difficult of circumstances and, once out of prison, lost that intense connection. With the dozens of prisoners I spoke to and got to know, one of the only things, perhaps *the* only thing they missed about prison was that intimate, daily, powerful connection to prisoner number 46664. I missed it too. But I knew also, as those men knew, that it could not be restored, that it was born of a certain time and place. And yet that did not take away from the power of the connection. Each of us keeps a small piece of him to ourselves.

In a curious way, in working with Mandela on his autobiography, I had to internalize him and his ideas. Many times I had to ask myself, "What would Nelson Mandela do?" It was a powerful exercise. It always made me, at least in those moments, a better person—calmer, more rational, more generous. I'd like to be able to say that those changes stayed with me; too often they slipped away. But Mandela's example remained with me, as I hope it will with you. As distant as his life's circumstances might be from our own, his example gives us something to hold on to, a set of principles and values that can guide us through difficult times.

One day, before Mary and I were married, Mandela said to her, "I give you my blessing because Richard is my son." I love that he called me one of his sons—and I loved him—but I also know that I have millions upon millions of brothers and sisters.

Acknowledgments

My route to this book—and to my now life-long connection to South Africa—was a serendipitous one. Susan Murcko and Jann Wenner took a chance and sent me to South Africa for *Rolling Stone* back in the mideighties, when the townships were burning. Alice Mayhew published a book that grew out of that magazine piece and did a superb job editing it. The ever-generous Dick Stolley gave a copy of that book to Bill Phillips, who was looking for a writer to collaborate with Nelson Mandela. Bill read the book overnight, called me the next day, and made me an offer I couldn't refuse. Bill was the wise and wonderful editor of Mandela's memoirs and the always delightful companion on that life-changing journey. Years later, my talented colleagues at *Time*—Romesh Ratnesar, Michael Elliott, Bobby Ghosh—urged me to write a cover story on Mandela for his ninetieth birthday. Josh Tyrangiel used his deft pen to lift up that piece beyond the ordinary.

For that piece as well as for this book, the extraordinary people at the Mandela Centre for Memory—Achmat Dangor, Verne Harris, Sahm Venter—have been extremely generous and knowledgeable. The great Ahmed Kathrada—who was at Mandela's side during those long years in prison—has enriched this book with his insight and, more important, his friendship.

My agent, Joy Harris, has been at my side during this entire time and has always provided stalwart support. My assistant, the incomparable Tosca LaBoy, has helped in a thousand different ways. Chris and Priscilla Whittle provided not only the most beautiful writing spot on the planet but their enduring friendship as well. My boss, John Huey, has enthusiastically supported this book and has taught me much about leadership in the bargain. And at *Time,* the peerless Ali Zelenko and her terrific PR team of Betsy Burton and Daniel Kile have done their usual superb job.

Rachel Klayman has been an extraordinarily thoughtful and creative editor whose attention to detail has improved this book in countless ways; I'd subject myself to her editing any time. Jenny Frost and Tina Constable have given unwavering support for this project, Penny Simon has worked wonders in the realm of publicity, and the entire team at Crown Publishers has been extremely dedicated.

I want to thank my wife, Mary, my eternal connection to South Africa, who in so many ways has been the inspiration for this book.

And, finally, for Gabriel and Anton, here's what the old man knows.

About the Author

Richard Stengel is the editor of *Time* magazine. He spent almost three years collaborating with Nelson Mandela on Mandela's bestselling and critically acclaimed autobiography, *Long Walk to Freedom*. He has written for many publications, including *The New Yorker* and *New York Times* and he is also the author of *January Sun: One Day, Three Lives, A South African Town*. He lives in New York with his wife, Mary Pfaff, and their two sons.